THE
KING JAMES
BIBLE

IN AMERICA

AN ORTHOGRAPHIC, HISTORICAL,
AND TEXTUAL INVESTIGATION

Bryan C. Ross

DISPENSATIONAL
PUBLISHING HOUSE, INC.

Scriptures quoted as KJV are taken from the KING JAMES VERSION (KJV).

Printed in the United States of America
ISBN: 978-1-945774-37-9

Dispensational Publishing House, Inc.
220 Paseo del Pueblo Norte
Taos, NM 87571

www.dispensationalpublishing.com

Ordering Information: Quantity sales. Special discounts are available on quantity purchases by churches, associations, and others. For details, contact the publisher at the address above.

Orders by U.S. trade bookstores and wholesalers. Please contact the publisher:
Tel: (844) 321-4202

2 3 4 5 6 7 8 9 10 1

To my wonderful wife Rebekah Ross without whose support projects like this would not be possible. I thank God for you everyday. Thank you for being an amazing help meet and friend.

Also, to my good friend and research partner David W. Reid. Thank you for forbearing with my many phone calls to discuss various aspects of this and other projects. You have been an example to many of how to deal gracefully with difficult circumstances. I thank God upon every remembrance of you. I am very grateful for the time the Lord has given us these past years.

Table of Contents

Introduction

BELIEVERS BEWARE OF COUNTERFEIT KING JAMES BIBLES![1]

IS IT A REAL KJV?[2]

So read the headlines on some pro-King James websites and publications. As these headlines suggest, some King James Bible Believers have expressed concern that modern printers of the King James Bible (KJB) such as Zondervan, Thomas Nelson, and Holman Bible Publishers, are taking liberties with the text. For example, Bibles produced on these presses change words like "throughly" in II Timothy 3:17 to "thoroughly"; or "alway" in Philippians 4:4 to "always"; or "ensample" in Philippians 3:17 to "example"; or "stablish" in Romans 16:25 to "establish." Some have gone so far as to assert that modern printings of the KJB exhibiting these spelling changes are "corruptions" on par with the changes made by modern versions.

---

1 Nic Kizziah. *Believers Beware of Counterfeit King James Bibles!*
http://www.biblebelievers.com/believers-org/counterfeit-kjv.html

2 Website has been removed subsequent to the writing of this paper.

Some view these changes as an attack of the adversary upon the final authority of God's written word.

It is believed by those making these assertions that words such as "thoroughly", "always", "example", and "establish" are different words, which have different meanings than their more archaic counterparts. In short, these changes are not viewed as simply orthographical updates in spelling; but as changes that substantively alter the meaning and doctrinal content of the Biblical text. Consequently, it has been posited by some, that believers who possess one of these modern printings of the KJB, do not possess the "pure word of God"; and need to purchase a copy of the King James text which is devoid of these changes in order to possess an uncorrupted copy of God's word in English.

The purpose of this small book is to investigate whether the words in question ("thoroughly", "always", "example", and "establish") are wholly different words with different meanings or simply differently spelled variants of the same word. These words have been chosen as emblems of a host of other words to which the same phenomena would apply. After an extensive study of the matter, I have become convinced it **is not true** that the words in question are wholly different words. Furthermore, I believe that to reason in this manner is detrimental to the position upholding the final authority of the KJB.

In order to substantiate this conclusion, I will present four basic lines of argumentation and evidence in two separate parts. Part I will discuss issues related to orthography and the text of the

KJB. First, it will be demonstrated that the pro-king James position as it is currently constituted, already acknowledges and accounts for variations in orthography between 1611 and 1769. Second, we will frame the discussion by looking at the challenge of *verbatim identicality*. It will be demonstrated that demanding "verbatim wording" not only reaches beyond the historical and textual evidence, but also creates an inconsistent and incoherent position, which cannot pass its own standard. Third, consideration will be given to the historic meanings of the words in question. This will be accomplished by considering a host of dictionaries and English language reference books stretching back to the early 17th century when the KJB was translated and published.

The fourth point, housed in Part II, will deal with the textual history of the KJB in the United States. Part II will demonstrate from history that American printings of the KJB were already making these orthographical changes for nearly a century before the publication of the Revised Version in 1881. From this it will be established that the existence of King James Bibles exhibiting these changes is not a recent phenomenon. The implications of this historical reality will also be examined.

As a King James Bible Believer, I have privately wrestled in recent years with how various details of the King James position have been messaged and articulated. Given that the current volume presents a new way of looking at the textual and historical data than has heretofore been enunciated; I am keenly aware there is a strong possibility my work will be misunderstood and/or mischaracterized.

In an effort to avoid these two misfortunes, the following points must be clear at the outset.

First, I am unequivocally a King James Bible Believer. I believe the KJB is God's word for English speaking people. God inspired his word and preserved it throughout history. The KJB is a formal equivalent (literal) translation of the preserved text into English. As such, I maintain the KJB and its underlying texts are inerrant in that they do not report anything about God's person, nature, character, creative acts, redemptive acts, or dispensational dealings with humanity; that is false. It is my position that the KJB contains all the correct readings and is without error in all that it reports.

Second, in endeavoring to accomplish its purpose; this volume critiques some of the teachings of fellow King James advocates. The work and/or writings of Matthew Verchuur (Bible Protector), Keith R. Blades, Kyle Stephens, and Local Church Bible Publishers have been utilized throughout as a means of framing the discussion. While in disagreement with the position posited by these men and/or ministries on certain points; I respect and commend them for their fine work in standing for the final authority of the KJB. I have personally benefited from the ministries of all four.

Finally, the goal of this book **is not** to take "the penknife of Jehudi" to my fellow King James Bible Believers for the purpose of sowing seeds of discord and division within an already attacked and maligned movement. Rather, I am concerned with the articulation of a clear and consistent position with respect to the KJB, which does not outstrip the historical and textual facts. It is to this end, for the clarity and consistency of our position; that the decision was made to draft this book. It is not productive for King James Bible Believers to assert things which can easily be proven inconsistent by further comprehensive study of the historical and textual facts.

Bryan C. Ross
Grace Life Bible Church
Grand Rapids, MI
September, 2019

Part I

Orthography and the King James Bible

A Brief Orthographic History of the King James Bible: 1611 to 1769

Critics of the KJB have maintained it is not inerrant on account of the fact that its text underwent numerous "revisions" between 1611 and 1769, when the current version of the text was first published. It is not uncommon for King James Bible Believers to be asked, "Which edition of the KJB is the inerrant one?" Historically, supporters of the KJB have been quick to point out that the only changes made to its text between 1611 and 1769 were either: 1) the correction of clear printer errors, 2) updates in orthography or the spelling of words, or 3) changes in punctuation as English grammar became more settled. Consequently, it is argued by King James advocates that these so-called "revisions" do not substantively alter the meaning or doctrinal content of the text; as do the far-reaching textual changes exhibited by the Critical Text and modern versions. While it is not entirely true that the only changes made to the King James text between 1611 and 1769 fall into the three categories identified above; the primary focus of this book is on the second category i.e., updates in orthography or the spelling of words.[3]

According to Noah Webster's *American Dictionary of the English Language* (1828), orthography is defined as:

1. The art of writing words with the proper letters, according to common usage.

2. The part of grammar which treats of the nature and properties of letters, and of the art of writing words correctly.

3. The practice of spelling or writing words with the proper letters.

In 1611, when the KJB was first published there was no standard or agreed upon orthography as to how English words should be spelled. Please consider the following examples from Genesis chapter 1. Note that only the first occurrence of a particular word is listed in the table.

---

3 In his ground breaking book *A Textual History of the King James Bible* (2004), Professor David Norton identifies over 1,500 textual variants (this number includes the Apocrypha) between the various editions of the KJB. In Appendix 8 on pages 200-355, Norton catalogues all the textual variants. While most of them are simply changes in spelling there are some differences in wording. Ultimately, none of these differences in wording are substantive or alter the doctrinal content of any passage but they do exist regardless of popular belief to the contrary. In 2011, I taught a lesson titled *Inerrancy and the King James Bible* in which I dealt with the findings gleaned from Norton's work. It was concluded that *verbatim identicality* of wording is not required because there are different ways of saying the same thing. If one were to demand *verbatim identicality* of wording with respect to the edition of the KJB one would indeed be forced to declare which particular edition of the KJB was the inerrant one to the exclusion of all the others.

Verse	1611 Spelling	1769 Spelling	Comments
Gen. 1:1	Heauen	heaven	Cap. in 1611 but not in 1769.
Gen. 1:2	forme	form	
	voyde	void	
	darkeneffe	darkness	f = s in the 1611
	vpon	upon	
	deepe	deep	
	mooued	moved	
Gen. 1:4	diuided	divided	
Gen. 1:5	euening	evening	
Gen. 1:7	vnder	under	
Gen. 1:9	appeare	appear	
Gen. 1:10	drie	dry	
Gen. 1:11	foorth	forth	
	grasse	grass	
	herbe	herb	
	yeelding	yielding	
	kinde	kind	
	it selfe	itself	One word in the 1769.
Gen. 1:14	bee	be	bee and be in the 1611.
	signes	signs	
	dayes	days	
	yeeres	years	
Gen. 1:15	giue	give	
Gen. 1:16	starres	stars	
Gen. 1:20	foorth	forth	
	aboundantly	abundantly	
	mouing	moving	
	foule	fowl	
	flie	fly	
	aboue	above	

Verse	1611 Spelling	1769 Spelling	Comments
Gen. 1:21	liuing	living	
	kinde	kind	
	winged	winged	
Gen. 1:22	fruitfull	fruitful	
Gen. 1:23	fift	fifth	
Gen. 1:24	cattell	cattle	
Gen. 1:26	vs	us	
	likenesse	likeness	
	aire	air	
	euery	every	
Gen. 1:27	owne	own	
	hee	he	
Gen. 1:28	mooueth	moveth	
Gen. 1:29	giuen	given	
	seede	seed	
Gen. 1:30	greene	green	

In addition, to the unsettled orthography illustrated by the above table, in some cases the 1611 spells the same word differently within the same verse or context. Consider the following few examples:

- bee (Genesis 1:14) v. be (Genesis 1:14)
- only (John 3:16) v. onely (John 3:18)
- commeth (John 3:31) v. cometh (John 3:31)
- kingdome (Mark 10:23) v. kingdom (Mark 10:24-25)

By 1769, the spellings of these words had become standardized and the text read accordingly: "be" (Genesis 1), "only"

(John 3), "cometh" (John 3), and "kingdom" (Mark 10). Despite the varied orthography exhibited above, these updates in spelling are commonly understood not to be substantive alterations of the doctrinal content of the text.

Other orthographical changes occurred in the English language between 1611 and 1769 such as how to handle the capitalization of words. For example, due to the influence of German (which capitalizes all nouns)[4] on the English language, the 1611 capitalizes many nouns that were not capitalized later on. Consider the following examples:

Passage	1611 Convention	1769 Convention
Matt 25:31 Angels v. Matt 25:41 angels	Capital A angel used for good angels; lower "a" used for bad angels	Lower case "a" used for all angels
Acts 27:9	Fast	fast
Acts 28:3	Viper	viper
Acts 28:9	Iland	island
Rom. 1:1	Gospel	gospel
Rom. 1:5	Apostleship	apostleship
Rom. 1:20	Creation	creation
Rom. 1:20	Power	power
Rom. 2:25	Circumcision	circumcision
Rom. 3:13	Aspes	aspes

These changes in capitalization are simply the movement of the English language away from the capitalization of nouns. Changes in capitalization rules are not actual changes in content. Such a change

---

4   The original 1611 was printed in Gothic typeface, which is Germanic in origin. It is thus not surprising that many nouns are capitalized in the 1611 consistent with German grammar.

is not a "revision" to a new word; it is simply a change in convention as to how to write the same word. Such changes are inconsequential as well as expected and understood by King James Bible Believers to be part of the normal orthographical development of the English language between 1611 and 1769.

Framing the Discussion: Confronting the Challenge of Verbatim Identicality

The idea that the four words "thoroughly", "always," "example," and "establish" are different and carry wholly different meanings from "throughly," "alway," "ensample," and "stablish" is of long-standing tradition among King James Bible Believers. This belief is based largely on what I have come to believe is an instance on the standard of *verbatim identicality* or the notion that any difference in wording of any kind constitutes a "corruption."

Until 2011, I believed that the only differences which existed between the 1611 and 1769 editions of the KJB, were the correction of printer errors as well as updates in punctuation and spelling. In May 2011, I was handed a copy of David Norton's 2004 book *A Textual History of the King James Bible*. The factual evidence presented by Norton was contrary to what I had been led to believe. There are differences between the various editions of the KJB that are not simply the correction of printer errors, updating of spelling, and punctuation.

In Appendix 8 of his book, Norton devotes 155 pages to chronicling 952 verses (this number does not include the Apocrypha) where differences in wording exist between 1611 and 1769 editions of the KJB. While many of these differences are related to orthography, there are also many cases where the various editions actually possess different words, additional words, or changes in word order. Please consider the following few examples:

Passage	1611	1769	Comment
Num. 3:13	"mine they shall be"	"mine shall they be"	
Num. 7:31	omits "of the weight"	adds "of the weight"	
Deut. 23:25	neighbors (plural)	neighbor (singular)	Singular/plural irrelevant in this context
I Ki. 6:1	fourscore	Eightieth	
II Ki. 15:15	"the conspiracy"	"his conspiracy"	Both read "which he made"
Ps. 24:3	"and"	"or"	
Zech. 4:2	"were"	"are"	It is a description of a vision and the verb tense is immaterial
Matt. 26:75	"words"	"word"	
Luke 19:9	"the son"	"a son"	Difference is immaterial in light of the word "also"
Jude 25	"now and ever."	"**both** now and ever."	The word "both" is inserted in the 1769 edition

Jude 25 stands out as an interesting case in point. The verse exhibits a wording difference between the 1611 and 1769 that goes beyond merely an update in spelling. The standard 1769 text contains an entire word that is not found in the 1611, the word "both." Does the inclusion of this word alter the substantive meaning of the text? If one answers yes, on the grounds that the verses are not identical in wording, then one would be forced to declare which edition of the KJB is the inerrant one, the 1611 or the 1769. This is the exact tactic used by critics of the KJB to try and entrap those who believe the KJB is without error. For the purposes of illustration please consider the following example. Is there any substantive difference in meaning between the following statements?

- I ate lunch with Ben and Charlie.
- I ate lunch with **both** Ben and Charlie.

There is no substantive difference in meaning between these two statements; rather, they are different ways of saying the same thing without exhibiting "verbatim wording." So, it is with Jude 25, as well as the rest of the examples provided in the table above.

In contrast, modern versions err because the wording is changed in a manner that alters the substantive doctrinal content/meaning of the text. For example, if either of the statements above read, "I ate lunch with Ben only;" this **would not** be a different way of saying the same thing but a substantive difference in meaning. Modern versions are full of these types of wording differences and omissions that if accepted, substantively change the Bible's content.

If preservation and inerrancy demand *verbatim identicality* of wording, then one is forced to determine which edition of the King James text is inerrant to the exclusion of all the others. It was while preparing to teach a seminar titled *Inerrancy and the King James Bible*, I came to understand that the nature of the differences is what matters in seeking to identify God's word. The realization came that there is a difference between 1) a different way of saying the same thing and 2) a substantive difference in meaning.[5]

Since 2011, I have come to believe that the observation regarding *verbatim identicality* has many and far reaching implications for the rest of the Bible version debate. These insights have brought clarity to the central topic being addressed in this book i.e., whether the words in question ("thoroughly", "always", "example", "establish") are wholly different words of discriminated meaning. If it could be demonstrated that their meaning is identical to their more archaic counterparts, then one must conclude that changing their orthography does not "corrupt" the text. We will now turn our attention toward a consideration of the meaning of the four of words in question.

---

5 The resources used to teach the seminar titled *Inerrancy and the King James Bible* can be accessed on the Grace Life Bible Church webpage at gracelifebiblechurch.com.

What Saith the Dictionary?

Over the years I have often heard in preaching or read in King James literature that words like "throughly" and "thoroughly" or "stablish" and "establish" are different words. In some cases, the audience/readers were told that if their KJB read "thoroughly" instead of "throughly" in II Timothy 3:17, their Bible was "corrupted." It was asserted that "throughly" was of entirely different meaning than "thoroughly." "Throughly" was defined as meaning "from the inside out or through you" as opposed to "thoroughly," which was defined as meaning something altogether different.

The notion that the words in question are different words, which carry entirely different meanings, is held by many King James Bible Believers. One such example is Matthew Verschuur, also known as Bible Protector out of Australia, who advocates for what he calls the Pure Cambridge Position. According to Brother Verschuur, only the circa 1900 Cambridge Text is totally free from errors of any kind and constitutes the pure word of God. In 2009, Bible Protector published a booklet titled *Glistering Truths: Distinctions in Bible Words* in which he argues that "every word and letter in the King James Bible is entirely accurate, that every jot and tittle is required for the exactness of the sense."[6]

In other words, if a single letter is out of place the text is incapable of conveying the exact sense. Consequently, Brother Verschuur maintains implicitly if not explicitly that any Bible that changes the spelling of "alway" to "always" or "ensample" to "example" is a "corrupted" Bible and not capable of expressing the exact sense of scripture. So, unless one possesses a particular printing (circa 1900) from a particular press (Cambridge University Press) they do not possess the pure word of God, according to Bible Protector.

While other King James Bible Believers would not insist that one possess a particular printing (circa 1900) from a particular press (Cambridge University Press) in order to have the pure word of God; they would agree with Bible Protector that editions which alter the spelling of the words in question are "perversions." Keith R. Blades' twelve-part series of videos on *A Brief Introduction to the Excellency of Older English* (*Excellency of Older English* hereafter) stands out as another prime example of this line of argumentation. As the title suggests, this series of studies discusses the merits of older English in terms of its precision and expressiveness for conveying the nuances of scripture.

For the record, I agree with Brother Blades' fundamental point. The older vocabulary and forms of early modern English exhibited by the KJB are far more precise and majestic in terms of conveying the

---

6 Matthew Verschuur. *Bible Protector*. http://www.bibleprotector.com.

truth of scripture than anything contemporary English has to offer. That being said, Brother Blades says certain things regarding the meaning of the words in question, which cannot be corroborated by any of the English language reference works he recommends or that I have been able to locate. Pastor Blades recommends the following English language reference works:

- *Oxford English Dictionary* 2nd Edition
- *American Dictionary of the English Language* by Noah Webster
- *An Etymological Dictionary of the English Language* by Rev. Walter W. Skeat
- *Crabb's English Synonyms* by George Crabb
- *Synonyms Discriminated* by Charles John Smith

Simply stated, I **am not** convinced that modern printings of the KJB, which utilize the updated spellings of these words are "perversions." This is due in large part to the fact English language dictionaries and reference works do not bear out that these words mean what Brother Blades and other Bible teachers have said they mean.

In preparation for this book, I consulted a lengthy list of English language reference books including dictionaries and compendiums of English synonyms. Some of these dictionaries date to the early 17th century and are contemporary with the translation work that was done between 1604 and 1611. As one can see the list of works consulted in preparation for this book far exceeds the number of references works recommended by Brother Blades. The list of works consulted includes the following:

- 1604—*A Table Alphabetical* by Robert Cawdrey
- 1616—*English Expositor* by John Bullokar[7]
- 1623—*English Dictionary* by Henry Cockeram
- 1656—*Glossographia* by Thomas Blount
- 1658—*New World of English Words* by Edward Phillips[8]
- 1676—*An English Dictionary* by Elisha Coles
- 1699—*Dictionary of the Terms Ancient and Modern of the Canting Crew* by B.E. Gent
- 1721—*An Universal Etymological English Dictionary* by Noah Bailey[9]
- 1755—*A Dictionary of the English Language* by Samuel Johnson
- 1818—*Crabb's English Synonyms* by George Crabb[10]
- 1828—*American Dictionary of the English Language* by Noah Webster

7   To view the 12th edition for 1719 visit: https://books.google.com/books?id=R8IDAAAAQ AAJ&printsec=frontcover&source=gbs_ge_summary_r&cad=0#v=onepage&q&f=false

8   To view the 3rd Edition from 1720 visit: https://archive.org/details/The_New_World_of_ English_Words_Or_A_General_Dictionary

9   To view a 1763 printing visit: https://archive.org/details/universaletymolo00bail

10   To view the enlarged 1st edition from 1826 visit: https://books.google.com/books?id=NZ tWAAAAcAAJ&printsec=frontcover&source=gbs_ge_summary_r&cad=0#v=onepage &q&f=false

- 1828—*A Dictionary of the English Language* by Samuel Johnson, John Walker, Robert S. Jameson (This is a British dictionary published the same year as Webster's work in America.)

- 1890—*Synonyms Discriminated: A Dictionary of Synonymous Words in the English Language* by Charles John Smith

- 1881—*An Etymological Dictionary of the English Language* by Rev. Walter W. Skeat[11]

- 1989—*Oxford English Dictionary* 2nd Edition[12]

After consulting the preceding list of reference books, I have concluded that the alleged differences in meaning between words like "throughly" and "thoroughly" have been completely fabricated. English language reference works simply do not support the idea that these words are different and of wholly different meaning. They have been read selectively by folks like Brother Blades to create the perception that the words don't mean the same thing. In most cases the words in their archaic form do not even appear in the majority of the references works listed above. When the archaic spellings do appear, readers either encounter the same definition offered for the modern spellings or instructions are given to see the entry for the modern form of the word.

11 To view the 2nd edition from 1883 visit: https://archive.org/stream/etymologicaldict00ske auoft#page/192/mode/2up

12 The first edition of the *Oxford English Dictionary* was produced in multiple volumes between the years of 1884 and 1928. The updated 3rd edition is available online for some entries.

We will now turn our attention to presenting the findings of the investigation into whether the words in question ("thoroughly", "establish", "always", and "example") are wholly different words with different meanings than their archaic counterparts. In order to accomplish this task, we will look at the following words throughout the duration of this chapter:

- "Throughly" and "Thoroughly"
- "Alway" and "Always"
- "Ensample(s)" and "Example(s)"
- "Stablish" and "Establish"

For each pair of words, I will present all of the relevant findings as well as offer some editorial comments on the nature of my work.

THROUGHLY AND THOROUGHLY

In his twelve-part video series on the *Excellency of Older English*, Keith R. Blades distinguished between the definitions of the words "thoroughly" and "throughly." Brother Blades stated that these two words are indicative of a "fine line of demarcation ... as they both express the issue of completeness, fullness, perfection, or lack of deficiency, or shortcoming in whatever they are talking about." Blades identified the fine line of demarcation as follows: "thoroughly views things from the outside; whereas throughly views things from the inside, or from the inside out so to speak." II Timothy 3:17 and I Thessalonians 2:13 are used to prove that "throughly" is describing an "inside out" type of work in the believer's inner man as opposed to an "outside" or external work demarcated by "thoroughly."[13] It is important to note that Pastor Blades does not cite even one English language reference work to support his assertion that a "fine line of demarcation" ever existed between the two words in question. While I do not dispute the doctrinal truth of I Thessalonians 2:13 regarding the working of God's word in the believer's inner man, the question at hand is, "does a difference between these two words exist as Brother Blades has asserted?"

If such a definitional difference exits, then one would be forced to declare which edition of the KJB is the inerrant one. This is based upon the textual FACTS stemming from the printed history of the KJB. Please consider the following table:

Passage	1611	1769	Changes Between Eds.
Gen. 11:3	*thorowly*	*throughly*	*thorowly → throughly*
Ex. 21:19	*throughly*	*thoroughly*	*throughly → thoroughly*
2Ki. 11:18	*throughly*	*thoroughly*	*throughly → thoroughly*
Job 6:2	*throughly*	*throughly*	
Ps. 51:2	*throughly*	*throughly*	
Jer. 6:9	*throughly*	*throughly*	
Jer 7:5	*throughly*	*throughly*	
Jer. 50:34	*throughly*	*throughly*	
Eze. 16:9	*throughly*	*throughly*	
Matt. 3:12	*throughly*	*throughly*	

13 Keith Blades. *A Brief Introduction to the Excellency of Older English*. Discussion of "thoroughly" and "throughly" begins at the 27:05 mark of the following video: https://youtu.be/0KJTI6cohH0?t=27m5s

Passage	1611	1769	Changes Between Eds.
Luke 3:17	*thorowly*	*throughly*	*thorowly* → *throughly*
II Cor. 11:6	*throughly*	*throughly*	
II Tim. 3:17	*throughly*	*throughly*	

The word "thorowly" occurs two times in the 1611 in Genesis 11:3 and Luke 3:17.

> 3 And † they layd one to another; Goe to. let vs make bricke, and † burne then thorowly And they had bricke for ſtone, and ſlime had they for morter.

Genesis 11:3
1769 reads throughly

> 17 whoſe fanne is in his hand, and he will throwly purge his floore, and will garner the wheat into his garner, but the chaffe he will burne with fire vnquencheable.

Luke 3:17
1769 reads throughly

> 19 If hee riſe againe, and walke a-broad vpon his ſtaffe, then ſhall hee that ſmote him, be quit : onely he ſhall pay for the loſſe of his time, and ſhall cauſe him to be throughly healed.

Exodus 21:19
1769 reads thoroughly

> 18 And all the people of the land went into the houſe of Baal, and brake it downe, his altars and his images brake they in pieces throughly, and ſlew Mat-tan the prieſt of Baal before the altars: and the Prieſt appointed † officers ouer the houſe of the LORD.

II Kings 11:18
1769 reads thoroughly

The *Oxford English Dictionary* (*OED*) identifies "thorowly" as the "obsolete spelling of thoroughly." Therefore, the 1611 originally read the equivalent of "thoroughly" in two places where the 1769 now reads "throughly." Likewise, the 1769 now reads "thoroughly" in two passages where the 1611 originally read "throughly." So if "throughly" and "thoroughly" have different meanings, as have been asserted, then either the 1611 or the 1769 is wrong in Exodus 21:19 and II Kings 11:18. In like manner, if "thoroughly" and "throughly" don't mean the same thing, then either the 1611 or the 1769 is wrong in Genesis 11:3 and Luke 3:17. The TEXTUAL FACTS are such that if these are truly different words of completely different meaning; than one must indeed choose which edition of the KJB is correct as critics have long argued.

Not only does the textual history of the KJB not bear out Pastor Blade's supposition, neither does any known English dictionary. The first hint of the word "throughly" found in an English dictionary occurs in *An Universal Etymological English Dictionary* from 1721 complied by Noah Bailey. Bailey's dictionary contains an entry for the word "through" for which the following definition is provided: "for thorough." So, from the earliest occurrence of the word "through" in a known English dictionary it is tied to the word "thorough."[14]

Moving forward in time, Noah Webster's *American Dictionary of the English Language* from 1828 defines "throughly" as follows:

> **THROUGHLY,** *adverb* thru'ly. Completely; fully; wholly. **1.** Without reserve; sincerely. [**For this, thoroughly is now used.**]

Webster says that "thoroughly" is now used for "throughly" and does not distinguish between them as did Brother Blades. This is truly puzzling on account of the fact that Blades recommends Webster's *American Dictionary* in his series on the *Excellency of Older English*. Likewise, the British publication *A Dictionary of the English Language*, also from 1828 possesses the following entry for "throughly."

THROUGHLY, See Thoroughly.

The *Oxford English Dictionary* follows suit by stating that "throughly" is an archaic form of "thoroughly." Please compare the *OED* entries for "throughly" and "thoroughly" side by side:

THROUGHLY, *adv. arch.*[15]	THOROUGHLY, *adv.*
[f. THROUGH *adv.* Or *adj.* + LY. **See also THOROUGHLY.**]	[f. THOROUGH adv. or adj. + LY, **See also THROUGHLY.**]
1. **Fully, completely, perfectly; = THOROUGHLY 2**	1. In a way that penetrates or goes through; right through; quite through. *Obs. rare.* With quots. 1637, 1703 cf. **THROUGHLY 2**
2. Through the whole thickness, substance, or extent; through, throughout, all through, quite through. *arch., poet.*	2. In a thorough manner or degree; In every part or detail; in all respects; with nothing left undone; **fully completely, wholly, entirely, perfectly.**
2b. Through, from beginning to end; for the whole length of time; all through. *Obs.*[16]	

15 Short for Archaic.

16 Short for Obsolete.

Please note that the *OED* clearly identifies "throughly" as an archaic word and tells its readers to "see also thoroughly." Moreover, the first definition offered for "throughly" explicitly tells the reader that "throughly" is equal to the second meaning of "thoroughly." Likewise, the entry for "thoroughly" instructs its readership to "see also throughly." Moreover, note that the first definition for "thoroughly" prompts its reader to cross-reference it with the second definition for "throughly." According to the *OED*, the two definitions offered for "thoroughly" are equal in meaning to the two primary definitions presented for "throughly" and vice versa. In short, these words constitute a difference without a distinction.

Another dictionary recommended by Blades, *An Etymological Dictionary of the English Language* (1881) by Rev. Walter W. Skeat contains the following entry for thorough: "going through and through, complete, entire. It is merely a later form of the prep. through. . . The use of the adj. probably arose from the use of throughly or thoroughly as an adj. in place of the adverbial use of through or thorough." In other words, yet another dictionary confirms there is no difference in meaning.

All the dictionaries that I consulted concerning the word "throughly" clearly state that it is an archaic form of "thoroughly." In short, the words are identical in meaning despite being spelled differently. The orthographical differences do not equate to a substantive difference in meaning. Moreover, there is no hint in any English language reference work of the "fine line of demarcation" between "throughly" and "thoroughly" taught by Pastor Blades.

Finally, on this point, his "demarcated" definitional distinction for "throughly" might work in II Timothy 3:17, but it breaks down when applied to other occurrences of the word elsewhere in the KJB. As we observed above, Blades defined "throughly" as viewing things from "the inside or from the inside out so to speak" whereas "thoroughly" viewed things from the "outside in." Let the word "throughly" in Genesis 11:3 serve as a case in point: "And they said one to another, Go to, let us make brick, and burn them **throughly**. And they had brick for stone, and slime had they for morter."

When they were burning bricks "throughly" to construct the Tower of Babel, were they burning them from the "inside out"? No, they threw them in a fire and burned them from the "outside in." Yet the 1769 text says "throughly" and not "thoroughly." Genesis 11:3 makes far more sense when one follows the dictionary definitions provided above for "throughly" over the unsubstantiated one offered by Pastor Blades. The bricks were burned "completely; fully; wholly"[17] or "through the whole thickness, substance, or extent"[18] not from the "inside out."

Maintaining that "throughly" and "thoroughly" are totally different words of entirely different meaning cannot be supported by English language reference books. More importantly, the unsubstantiated discriminated meanings enunciated by Blades cannot be consistently applied across the totality of the Biblical text. Therefore, it is detrimental to one's belief in the inerrancy of the KJB to argue

---

17 Noah Webster's *American Dictionary of the English Language*

18 *Oxford English Dictionary*

that there is. If one wishes to persist in this position, they would be forced logically to declare which edition of the KJB is the inerrant one, the 1611 or the 1769. King James advocates need not to adopt positions that play into the hands of our critics and can easily be proven wrong by anyone familiar with the textual history of the KJB.

ALWAY AND ALWAYS

Many King James Bible Believers also see a difference in meaning between the words "alway" and "always." The Bible Protector, Matthew Verschuur ascribes the following difference to these two words in his booklet, *Glistering Truths: Distinctions in Bible Words*:

> The word "always" means "at every time" and "on every occasion." Whereas the word "alway" means "all the time" and "perpetually." For example, Jesus said, "lo, I am with you alway, *even unto the end of the world. Amen.*" (Matthew 28:20b). Yet He also said, "but me ye have not always." (John 12:8b). This is not a contradiction, since John is describing Jesus' personal physical presence. Even though Jesus is not "always" on Earth by His own physical person, yet He is "alway" with His people on the Earth by the Holy Ghost.[19]

Bible Protector makes no mention of the fact that the same Greek word translated "always" in John 12:8 is elsewhere rendered "ever" six times, "alway" five times, and "evermore" two times by the King James Translators. Please also note that no English language resource is given to substantiate the difference between the two words.

---

19 Matthew Verschuur. *Glistering Truths.* 19.

One is simply asked to take Brother Verschuur's word for it. "Alway" and "always" appear to be another distinction without a difference.

Keith R. Blades also distinguishes between the two words in his series on the *Excellency of Older English*. He does not, however, make the same distinction as Bible Protector. This time, to support the notion that "alway" means "all the way," Blades references the *Oxford English Dictionary*. Regarding this matter Blades states:

> . . . it (the word "alway") is still there in English dictionaries that trace the etymology of words. Unfortunately, most modern English dictionaries if they even list the word alway will simply list it as archaic obsolete and simply tell you that it means the same thing as always. But that is not case at all as we indicated last time. An English dictionary like the *Oxford English Dictionary*, a very thorough English dictionary that deals with the etymology of words; and the historical development and use of words and also is very discriminating when it comes to words that are assumed to be synonymous and are certainly not the case at all. A dictionary like that makes it plain and clear that the word alway, though not utilized today as a single word itself did not mean what the word always means. . . "Alway is a shortened form of the expression "all the way." Alway is describing the fact that there is a prescribed course so to speak or something that has identifiable parameters to it. It has a commencement to it and an objective at the end or termination to it. Alway as a contractor form of the statement "all the way" is describing the issue of the progress along that prescribed course or along those parameters and describing the effect of something throughout that parameter.[20]

---

20 Keith R. Blades. *The Excellency of Older English*. Discussion of "alway" and "always" begins at the 11:12 mark of the following video: https://youtu. be/0KJTI6cohH0?t=11m12s . To hear Blades' comments on the *OED* please listen to the first 5 minutes of Lesson 3 to the series at the following link: http://www.enjoythebible. org/excellency-of-older-english/

Brothers Blades and Verschuur both believe that there is a "discriminated" difference between "alway" and "always" but for different reasons. Likewise, they do not agree as to what the difference in meaning actually is.

Since Pastor Blades referenced the *OED* entry to support his "discriminated" definition we will deal with that dictionary first. Please note, however, that the word "alway" does not appear in any of the dictionaries identified above until the 19th century with Noah Webster's *American Dictionary of the English Language* in 1828. It is true that the *OED* states that "alway" was originally a shortened form of the two words "ALL and WAY" and that its meaning was associated with the concept of "all the way," as Brother Blades purports in his teaching. That being said, he selectively quotes the *OED* to prove his point and does not give his audience the full definition. The entry cited by Pastor Blades reads as follows in the 2nd edition of the *OED*:[21]

> **ALWAY**, *adv.*
>
> [orgi. two words ALL and WAY, in the accusative of space or distance = *all the way*, *the whole way*, probably at first in reference to space traversed, **but already in oldest Eng. transferred to an extent of time,** *all along*, *all the time*, *continually*. Afterwards confused with the genitive form, **ALWAYS, which has superseded it in prose, alway surviving only in poetry or as an archaism.**] [emphasis mine]
>
> 1. All along, all the time, perpetually, throughout all time.

---

21 This would have been the most recent edition of the *OED* available to Blades at the time he was teaching.

2. = ALWAYS 1; every time, at all times, on all occasions. Opposed to *sometimes, occasionally.*

3. In any case, after all, still. = ALWAYS 3. *Obs.*

The bolded sections above highlight the critical pieces of the *OED* that Brother Blades fails to share with his audience. While the word "alway" was at one time a reference to "space traversed" i.e., "all the way;" the meaning of "alway" was already even in "**oldest English** transferred to an extent of time, *all along, all the time, continually,"* an interesting omission on Blades' part, given the title of his series of studies. Second, the *OED* states that "always" superseded "alway" in prose and that the use of "alway" only survives in poetry "or as an archaism." In other words, "alway" is an archaic form of "always," the exact opposite point of what Brother Blades is asserting.

A more recent addition of the *OED*, the updated 3rd Edition, has completely dropped the bracketed statement above originally cited by Brother Blades. Furthermore, the connection between "alway" and "always" is further strengthened in the current edition of the *OED*. Please consider the following entries side by side:

Alway	Always
After the Middle English period alway becomes increasingly less common in standard English, being supplanted in all senses by always adv. By the 19th cent. the word survives mainly in literary and regional uses.

1. = always adv. 3.

2. = always adv. 1.

3. †a. = always adv. 2b. Obs.

b. = always adv. 2a. See also (alway) foreseen or foreseeing that at foresee v. 4. | 1. On all occasions, at all times; on every occasion, every time; (sometimes with the implication of annoyance) repeatedly, over and over.

2. a. At any rate; at all events; in any case; anyway, anyhow. In later use esp.: if nothing else; as a last resort.

†b. Nevertheless; despite this; still. Obs.

3. For all time, forever; for or throughout a long period; continually, perpetually, without any interruption. |

Careful readers will notice that every entry for "alway" is equal to one of the definitions offered for "always," according to the *OED*. Consequently, there is little reason to view these words as possessing a "discriminated" difference in meaning as has been asserted by many King James advocates.

Matters are further compounded when one considers the historical examples of the use of "alway" provide in the *OED*. Underneath the first definition, "for all time, forever; for or throughout a long period; continually, perpetually, without any interruption" the *OED* provides Matthew 28:20 as an example: "Teaching them to observe all things whatsoever I have commanded you: and, lo, I am with you **alway,** *even* unto the end of the world. Amen."

The very dictionary Pastor Blades references to support his point tells its readers that the word "alway" in Matthew 28:20 means "all along, all the time, throughout all time" not "all the way" as he asserted.[22] Likewise, the *OED* ascribes John 7:6 as an example of the second definition which is explicitly stated to equal "always" i.e., "On all occasions, at all times; on every occasion, every time." John 7:6 states: "Then Jesus said unto them, My time is not yet come: but your time is **alway** ready".

So according to the examples provided by the *OED* "alway" is an archaic form of "always." Moreover, the *OED* definitions for "alway" and "always" have more in common with each other than they do with the "discriminated" definition provided by Brother Blades as a result of his selective usage of an earlier edition of the *OED*. Simply stated, the *OED*, regardless of the edition, does not support Blades' teaching; it disproves it.

The *OED* is not the only dictionary to support the notion that "alway" is an archaic form of "always" and that they are different ways of saying the same thing, not words of entirely different meaning. Noah Webster's *American Dictionary of the English Language* contains the following entry for "Al'way or Al'ways:"

> **AL'WAY or AL'WAYS**, adverb [*all* and *way*; Sax. *Eal*, and *weg*, way; properly, a going, at all going; hence, at all times.]
>
> 1. Perpetually; throughout all time; as, God is always the same.
>
> 2. Continually; without variation.
>
> I do alway those things which please him. John 8. Mat. 28.

---

22 This is true in the updated 3rd Edition as well.

3. Continually or constantly during a certain period, or regularly at stated intervals.

Mephibosheth shall eat bread alway at my table. 2 Sam. 9.

4. At all convenient times; regularly.

Cornelius prayed to God alway. Acts 10. Luke 18. Eph. 6.

Alway is now seldom used. The application of this compound to time proceeds from the primary sense of way, which is a going or passing; hence, continuation.

Noah Webster provides the exact same definition for "always" that he provided for "alway."

So according to both the *OED* and Noah Webster's *American Dictionary of the English Language* it is not appropriate or accurate to maintain that "alway" and "always" are different words of entirely different meaning. "Always" is the modern form of the archaic word "alway." *An Etymological Dictionary of the English Language* (1881) by Rev. Walter W. Skeat, another dictionary recommended by Blades, combines the words "alway" and "always" in the same entry and defines both of them as meaning "for ever."

With these observations from the dictionary in mind, it is clear that the King James translators viewed the words "alway" and "always" as interchangeable terms. The English word "alway" occurs eleven times in eleven verses in the King James Old Testament. There are four different Hebrews words that are rendered "alway" in English: *tamiyd, yowm, `owlam,* and *netsach.* In every case without fail there are instances where the same Hebrew word is rendered "always" elsewhere in the Old Testament. Please consider the following tables;

occurrences of "alway" have been italicized to make them standout. Note that the tables below are not intended to be exhaustive.

tamiyd (H8548)[23]	English Translation	*yowm* (H3117)[24]	English Translation
Ex. 25:30	*alway*	Deut. 5:29	*always*
Ex. 27:20	*always*	Deut. 6:24	*always*
Ex. 38:30	*continually*	Deut. 11:1	*alway*
Num. 9:16	*alway*	Deut. 14:23	*always*
Deut. 11:12	*always*	Deut. 28:33	*alway*
II Sam. 9:10	*alway*	I Kn. 11:36	*alway*
Ps. 16:8	*always*	II Kn. 8:19	*alway*
Pro. 5:19	*always*	II Ch. 18:7	*always*
Pro. 28:14	*alway*		
Eze.38:8	*always*		

23 The Hebrew word *tamiyd* occurs 104 times in 103 verses in the Masoretic Text supporting the KJB. Of these 104 occurrences the Hebrew word was translated as follows by the King James translators: continually (53x), continual (26x), daily (7x), always (6x), always (4x), ever (3x), perpetual (2x), continual employment (1x) evermore (1x), and never (1x). To view the full Lexicon entry for *tamiyd* visit: https://www.blueletterbible.org/lang/lexicon/lexicon.cfm?Strongs=H8548&t=KJV

24 The Hebrew word *yowm* occurs 2,287 times in 1,9831 verses in the Masoretic Text supporting the KJB. Of these 2,287 occurrences the Hebrew is rendered in English as follows by the King James translators: day (2,008x), time (64x), chronicles (with H1697) (37x), daily (44x), year (14x), continually (10x), when (10x), as (10x), while (8x), full (8x), always (4x), whole (4x), alway (4x), misc. (44x). To view the full Lexicon entry for *yowm* visit: https://www.blueletterbible.org/lang/lexicon/lexicon.cfm?Strongs=H3117&t=KJV

`owlam (H5769)[25]	English Translation	netach (5331)[26]	English Translation
Gen. 6:3	*always*	Ps. 9:18	*alway*
I Ch. 16:15	*always*	Ps. 103:9	*always*
Job 7:16	*alway*	Isa. 57:16	*always*
Ps. 119:112	*alway*		
Jer. 20:17	*always*		

All four of these Hebrew words carry meanings that agree with the definitions presented in the English dictionaries surveyed above (See lexicon information provided in the footnotes.).[27] It should also be noted that the same Hebrew word (*tamiyd*) appears in both II Samuel 9:7 as well as in verse 10. The end of verse 7 reads, ". . . and thou shalt eat bread at my table **continually**." The English word "continually" answers to the Hebrew word *tamiyd* where in verse 10 the translators rendered the same Hebrew word as "alway:" ". . . shall eat bread **alway** at my table."

---

25   The Hebrew word `owlam occurs 439 times in 414 verses in the Masoretic Text support-ing the KJB. Of these 439 occurrences the Hebrew word is translated as follows by the King James Translators: ever (272x), everlasting (63x), old (22x), perpetual (22x), ever-more (15x), never (13x), time (6x), ancient (5x), world (4x), always (3x), alway (2x), long (2x), never (with H408) (2x), misc. (6x). To view the full Lexicon entry for `owlam visit: https://www.blueletterbible.org/lang/lexicon/lexicon.cfm?Strongs=H5769&t=KJV

26   The Hebrew word *netsach* occurs 43 times in 42 verses in the Masoretic Text support-ing the KJB. Of these 43 occurrences the Hebrew word is rendered in English as follows by the King James translators: ever (24x), never (4x), perpetual (3x), always (2x), end (2x), victory (2x), strength (2x), alway (1x), constantly (1x), evermore (1x), never (with H3808) (1x). To view the full Lexicon entry for *netsach* visit: file:///C:/Users/King-James1611/Dropbox/KJB Class/Throughly/netsach

27   View the definitions for each Hebrew word by visiting the links provided in the footnotes for each word.

- II Samuel 9:7—And David said unto him, Fear not: for I will surely shew thee kindness for Jonathan thy father's sake, and will restore thee all the land of Saul thy father; and thou shalt eat bread at my table **continually** (*tamiyd*).

- II Samuel 9:10—Thou therefore, and thy sons, and thy servants, shall till the land for him, and thou shalt bring in *the fruits*, that thy master's son may have food to eat: but Mephibosheth thy master's son shall eat bread **alway** (*tamiyd*) at my table. Now Ziba had fifteen sons and twenty servants.

It is clear that the King James translators viewed "alway" and "always" as synonyms, both of which mean "continually," as both the *OED* and Noah Webster asserted. The translators did not see these words as possessing some sort of "discriminated difference." They are different ways of saying the same thing.

A similar picture unfolds when one considers occurrences of the English word "alway" in the New Testament. "Alway" occurs twelve times in twelve verses in the King James New Testament. Just as we saw with the Hebrew words in the Old Testament the various Greek words in the New Testament rendered "alway" are also translated "always" elsewhere in the New Testament. The lone exception is the occurrence of "alway" in Matthew 28:20.[28]

---

28 In Matthew 28:20 "alway" in English corresponds with the Greek words *pas* and *hēmera*.

pantote (G3842)[29]	English Translation	*diapantos* (G1275)[30]	English Translation	*Aei* (G104)[31]	English Translation
Mat. 26:11	*always (2x)*	Mk. 5:5	*always*	Act. 7:51	*always*
Mk. 14:7	*always*	Act. 10:2	*alway*	II Cor. 4:11	*alway*
Lk. 18:1	*always*	Act. 24:16	*always*	II Cor. 6:10	*alway*
Jhn. 7:6	*alway*	Rom. 11:10	*alway*	Tit. 1:12	*alway*
Jhn. 8:29	*always*	Heb. 9:6		Heb. 3:10	*alway*
Jhn. 11:42	*always*			I Pet. 3:15	*always*
Jhn. 12:8	*always (2x)*			II Pet. 1:12	*always*
Rom. 1:9	*always*				
I Cor. 1:4	*always*				
I Cor. 15:58	*always*				
II Cor. 2:14	*always*				
II Cor. 4:10	*always*				
II Cor. 5:6	*always*				
II Cor. 9:8	*always*				
Gal. 4:18	*always*				
Eph. 5:20	*always*				
Phl. 1:4	*always*				
Phl. 1:20	*always*				

29 The Greek word *pantote* occurs 42 times in 38 verses in the Greek text supporting the KJB. According to *Strong's Concordance* the Greek word *pantote* means: "at all times, always, ever." The Greek word was variously rendered in English as follows by the King James translators: always (29x), ever (6x), alway (5x), and evermore (2x). To view the full Lexicon entry for *pantote* visit: https://www.blueletterbible.org/lang/lexicon/lexicon.cfm?Strongs=G3842&t=KJV

30 The Greek word *diapantos* occurs 7 times in 7 verses in the Greek text supporting the KJB. The Greek word was variously translated by the King James translators as: always (3x), alway (2x), and continually (2x). To view the full Lexicon entry for *diapantos* visit: https://www.blueletterbible.org/lang/lexicon/lexicon.cfm?Strongs=G1275&t=KJV

31 The Greek word *aei* occurs 7 times in 7 verses in the Greek text supporting the KJB. The Greek word was variously rendered with the following English words by the King James translators: alway (4x), always (3x), and ever (1x). To view the full Lexicon entry for *aei* visit: https://www.blueletterbible.org/lang/lexicon/lexicon.cfm?Strongs=G104&t=KJV

pantote (G3842)[29]	English Translation	*diapantos* (G1275)[30]	English Translation	*Aei* (G104)[31]	English Translation
Phl. 2:12	*always*				
Phl. 4:4	*alway*				
Col. 1:3	*always*				
Col. 4:6	*alway*				
Col. 4:12	*always*				
I Thes. 1:2	*always*				
I Thes. 2:16	*alway*				
I Thes. 3:6	*always*				
II Thes. 1:3	*always*				
II Thes. 1:11	*always*				
II Thes. 2:13	*alway*				
Phm. 1:4	*always*				

According to *Strong's Concordance* the Greek word *pantote* from the left-hand column above means: "at all times, always, ever." The definition is precisely the meaning of the English words "alway" and "always" according to both the *OED* and the *American Dictionary of the English Language* by Noah Webster. The same could be said for the meanings of the Greek words *diapantos* and *aei* identified above.[32]

Making these translational and definitional observations begs the question of why did the King James translators not just render

---

32 The Greek word *diapantos* means "constantly, always, continually," according to *Strong's Concordance*. Likewise, *aei* is defined as meaning: 1) perpetually, incessantly; and 2) invariably, at any and every time: when according to the circumstances something is or ought to be done again.

Hebrew and Greek words in English in a uniform manner with the same English word all the time? The translators themselves have left us with an explanation for this reality in the Preface to the 1611. In "The Translators to the Reader" the translators explain the nature and scope of the translation process they utilized when conducting their work. According to the Preface, The King James translators did not employ a principle of rigidity when taking words from the donor language (Hebrew/Greek) and rendering them in the receptor language (English) which means that in the minds of the translators there are multiple acceptable ways of saying the same thing.

> Another thing we think good to admonish thee of, gentle reader that we have not tied ourselves to an uniformity of phrasing, or to an identity of words, as some peradventure would wish that we had done, because they observe, that some learned men somewhere, have been as exact as they could that way. Truly, that we might not vary from the sense of that which we had translated before, if the word signified that same in both places (for there be some words that be not the same sense everywhere) we were especially careful, and made a conscience, according to our duty. But, that we should express the same notion in the same particular word; as for example, if we translate the Hebrew or Greek word once by PURPOSE, never to call it INTENT; if one where JOURNEYING, never TRAVELING; if one where THINK, never SUPPOSE; if one where PAIN, never ACHE; if one where JOY, never GLADNESS, etc. Thus to mince the matter, we thought to savour more of curiosity than wisdom, and that rather it would breed scorn in the Atheist, than bring profit to the godly Reader. For is the kingdom of God to become words or syllables? Why should we be

in bondage to them if we may be free, use one precisely when we may use another no less fit, as commodiously?[33]

In other words, as long as an English word fits the sense of the Hebrew or Greek in a given passage; the King James translators did not lock themselves into rendering a given word from the donor language with the same word in the receptor language every time. This was done on purpose by the translators, so as to enrich the translation despite their knowledge that some would take issue with the practice.[34]

The words "*alway*" and "*always*" do not differ substantively in meaning. They constitute a distinction without a difference. Updating the orthography of "*alway*" to "*always*" does not create a substantive difference in meaning on par with those exhibited by modern versions. Rather Bibles exhibit these spelling changes have simply sought to employ modern spelling conventions consistently.

ENSAMPLE(S) AND EXAMPLE(S)

Much has been made by King James Bible Believers of the alleged difference between the words "ensample" and "example." Entire sermons have been preached highlighting the difference between these two words. Bible Protector, Matthew Verschuur

---

33 Preface: The Translators to the Reader from the 1611 edition.

34 In the Preface, the King James translators acknowledge that the Puritans would not like the inclusion of "old Ecclesiastical words" in the new translation. "Lastly, we have on the one side avoided the scrupulosity of the Puritans, who leave the old Ecclesiastical words, and betake them to other, as when they put WASHING for BAPTISM, and CONGRE-GATION instead of CHURCH. . ."

maintains that there is a difference in meaning between these two words:

> "An "example" is an outward sample, while an "ensample" is one that can be internalized through specific personal knowledge of the object looked at.
>
> "Brethren, be followers together of me, and mark them which walk so as ye have us for an ensample." (Philippians 3:17)."[35]

Once again, please note that Brother Verschuur does not reference any English language reference book to support these statements.

My search of 17th and 18th century dictionaries for the word "ensample" turned up some interesting findings. Two early English dictionaries contained entries for the word "ensample." Edward Philipps' *New World of Words* originally published in 1658 contains the entry for the word:

ENSAMPLE (old world) an example, model, or pattern.

In like manner, Noah Bailey's *An Universal Etymological English Dictionary* from 1721 defines "ensample" as "example or pattern." According to some of the earliest known English dictionaries the word "ensample" is an "old world" way of saying "example." These dictionaries do not present a discriminated or nuanced meaning between the two words.

The same could be said for prominent English dictionaries of the 19th and 20th centuries as well. Noah Webster's famous

---

35 Matthew Verschuur. *Glistering Truths*. 28.

American Dictionary of the English Language from 1828 defines "ensample" as follows:

> **ENSAMPLE**
>
> **Ensample**, *noun* [Latin exemplum.] An example; a pattern or model for imitation.
>
> Being ensamples to the flock. 1 Peter 5:3.
>
> Ensample, *verb transitive* To exemplify; to shew by example. **This word is seldom used, either as a noun or a verb. [See Example.]**

According to Webster, the word "ensample" is seldom used and means "an example, a pattern or model for imitation." Not only is this definition identical to those offered in 17th and 18th centuries dictionaries but readers of Webster are explicitly told to see the word "example" for further clarification.[36] Walter W. Skeat's *An Etymological Dictionary of the English Language* from 1881 informs its readers similarly. Skeat defines "ensample" as "an example" and tells his readers to "see Example."

The *Oxford English Dictionary* presents similar findings in an expanded format. The *OED* clearly identifies the word "ensample" as an archaic form of the word "example."

> **ENSAMPLE**, n. *arch.*
>
> =EXAMPLE in various senses.
>
> The mod. archaistic use is almost whole due to reminisce of the

---

36 To read Webster's entry for "example" visit: http://webstersdictionary1828.com/Dictionary/example

passages in which the word occurs in the New Testament. In four of these passages it is used in sense 2, and is retained unaltered in the R.V.; in the remaining two it has sense 3, and has in the R.V. been replaced by example.

1. An illustrative instance.

†b. quasi-*adv.* = 'for example'. *Obs.*

2. A precedent which may be followed or imitated; a pattern or model of conduct.

b. Phrases: +*in (+to) ensample; to give, set (an) ensample; to take ensample (+at, by, of).*

†c. *in ensample*: after the model (*of*); in imitation of the fact (that). *Obs.*

3. A deterrent instance of punishment, or of the evil consequences of any course of conduct; a practical warning. Const. *to, of* (the person to be warned), also with possessive pronoun. Phrases, *for,* †*in ensample.*[37]

Twice in this definition there is a †sign directing the reader to an additional obsolete (*Obs.*) entry for "ensample." That entry is for the verb "ensample."

†**ENSAMPLE,** v. *Obs.*

[f. prec. N.]

1. *trans.* a. To authorize by example; also, to set forth as an example.

b. To give an example or instance of.

2. To give an example to; to instruct by example. Also to model (something, oneself) *by, upon.*

b. *intr.* To give an example (to).

---

37 *OED 2nd Ed.*

In summation, neither the *OED* nor the earlier English diction-aries identified above support the nuanced definition of "ensample" offered by Bible Protector in *Glistering Truths*. The words "ensample" and "example" do not differ substantively. Rather they are synonymous in meaning contrary to the claims of some King James Bible Believers.

The synonymous nature of "ensample" and "example" is further confirmed by a consideration of how the King James translators handled these words when doing their work. First, the word(s) "ensample(s)" do not appear anywhere in the King James Old Testament. In the New Testament there are two different Greek words that are translated "ensample(s)" by the King James translators: 1) the Greek word *typos* and 2) the Greek word *hypodeigma*. Both of these Greek words are translated as either "ensample(s)" or "example(s)" in English throughout the New Testament by the translators. Once again for sake of visual clarity, the older spelling is placed in italic within the following table.

typos (G5179)[38]	English Translation	*hypodeigma* (G5262)[39]	English Translation
I Cor. 10:6	*examples*	Jhn. 13:15	*example*
I Cor. 10:11	*ensamples*	Heb. 4:11	*example*
Phl. 3:17	*ensample*	Heb. 8:5	*example*

---

38 The Greek word *typos* occurs 16 times in 15 verses in the Greek text supporting the KJB. Of these occurrences the King James translators variously rendered the Greek word as follows: ensample(s) (5x), print (2x), example(s) (3x), pattern (2x), fashion (1x), manner (1x), and form (1x). To view the full Lexicon entry for *typos* visit: https://www.blueletterbible.org/lang/lexicon/lexicon.cfm?Strongs=G5179&t=KJV

39 The Greek word *hypodeigma* occurs 6 times in 6 verses in the *Textus Receptus*, the Greek text supporting the KJB. Of these 6 occurrences the King James rendered *hypodeigma* in English as: example (4x), pattern (1x), and ensample (1x). To view the full Lexicon entry for *hypodeigma* visit: https://www.blueletterbible.org/lang/lexicon/lexicon.cfm?Strongs=G5262&t=KJV

typos (G5179)[38]	English Translation	*hypodeigma* (G5262)[39]	English Translation
I Thes. 1:7	*ensamples*	Jam. 5:10	*example*
I Thes. 4:12	*example*	II Pet. 2:6	*ensample*
II Thes. 3:9	*ensample*		
Heb. 8:5	*example*		
I Pet. 5:3	*ensamples*		

Other Greek words are also translated "example" by the King James translators but only the words *typos* and *hypodeigma* are ever rendered as "ensample(s)." Given these facts it is evident that the translators viewed them as interchangeable terms and not having discriminated differences.

At the beginning of this section we observed that Brother Verschuur argues that "ensample" and "example" do not mean the same thing. Specifically, he stated, "An 'example' is an outward sample, while an 'ensample' is one that can be 'internalized through specific personal knowledge of the object looked at.'"[40] This distinction is not supported by the English language references books we have surveyed in this section. Moreover, the alleged difference would once again make for an awkward reading of certain passages if applied consistently to the Biblical text.

According to Bible Protector, one must have "specific personal knowledge" of a thing in order for it to constitute an "ensample." In contrast, an "example" is simply an "outward sample" not requiring internalization through "specific personal knowledge." The problem with this is that the same things are described as being both "examples"

40 Matthew Verschuur. *Glistering Truths*. 28.

and "ensamples" in the New Testament. Consider for a moment that the destruction of Sodom and Gomorrah is said to be an "ensample" in II Peter 2:6; as well as an "example" in Jude 7. Given Brother Verschuur's definitions, it makes sense that Sodom and Gomorrah could be an "example" to Jude's readership because "specific personal knowledge" is not required to qualify as an "example." However, it **does not** make sense that Sodom and Gomorrah could have also been an "ensample," because Peter's readers lacked the "specific personal knowledge" necessary for these Old Testament events to constitute an "ensample." Therefore, the events of Sodom and Gomorrah could not serve as an "ensample" for Peter's readership, according to the definition provided by Brother Verschuur. Yet, II Peter 2:6 says that Sodom and Gomorrah was an "ensample." Bible Protector's asserted definitions cannot be reconciled with the text of scripture.

Once again, a manufactured definitional difference between words places two Biblical texts at odds with each other. The same could be said for those who were "overthrown in the wilderness" in I Corinthians 10; for the events in the wilderness are spoken of being both an "example" and an "ensample" in the same context. It makes far more sense to view the two words in question as synonyms than to subscribe to the alleged "discriminated" difference between them. The same Greek word appears twice in I Corinthians 10, once in verse 6 and again in verse 11.

- I Corinthians 10:6—Now these things were our examples (*typos*), to the intent we should not lust after evil things, as they also lusted.

- I Corinthians 10:11—Now all these things happened unto them for ensamples (*typos*): and they are written for our admonition, upon whom the ends of the world are come.

Again, it makes far more sense to view this example in I Corinthians 10 as an instance where the translators elected to variously render the same Greek word via two English words of synonymous meaning; than it does to manufacture a meaning for "ensample," which doesn't make sense given the parameters of the alleged definitional difference.

Kyle Stevens is another prominent example of an author arguing for a substantive difference in meaning between "example" and "ensample." In Chapter 9, "Ensamples are not Examples," of his book *The Certainty of the Words: How the King James Bible Resolves the Ambiguity of the Original Languages*, Brother Stephens argues that while the words are similar to each other they are NOT substantively equivalent in meaning. Stephens endeavors to establish the discriminated substantive difference between the two words via the KJB alone. There is but one reference to a dictionary entry for "ensample" from Noah Webster's *American Dictionary of the English Langue* (See citation above on pages 45-46). Regarding this entry, Stephens states: "the case of ensample(s) not being the same as example(s), though all the new versions and scholars make them so, has been clearly demonstrated in this chapter. Even Webster, in his English dictionary masterpiece of 1828, makes the two words essentially equivalent."[41]

---

41   Kyle Stephens. *The Certainty of the Words: How the King James Bible Resolves the Ambiguity of the Original Languages*. 367.

Simply stated, Brother Stephens does not agree with Noah Webster's reporting of the words' substantive equivalence.

After surveying all the occurrences of "example(s)" in the New Testament, Stephens provides the following definition which he gleaned exclusively from the KJB:

> In the King James Bible, an *example* serves as a warning or a pattern for those who are not in the exact predicament or scenario. An *example* is a pattern of behavior that is not necessarily intended to be exactly mimicked or emulated or precisely repeated, but a lesson drawn from and even extended to apply to other unrelated exercises. An *example* is a pattern, behavior or occurrence that is to be learned from, and lessons drawn from, but not necessary identically copies or reproduced."[42]

Please note that this definition derived from the KJB by Brother Stephens does not match the meaning provide by any known English Langue resource nor does it match the discriminated definition of an "example" provided by Bible Protector at the outset of this section.

Later in Chapter 9, Stephens surveys all the occurrences of the word "ensample(s)" in the New Testament. While doing so, he provides the following discriminated meaning for "ensample(s)" as opposed to "example(s):"

> *Examples* in the scriptures are loosely fitted lessons, warning and applications. They cannot be copied or emulated precisely due to certain boundaries or constraints of circumstance. *Ensamples* are to be followed as precisely and as ex-

---

42   Ibid., 356.

actly as possible. They are literally the samples of how we should live, respond or act.[43]

At the conclusion to his discussion of the word "ensample(s)" one finds the following summative statements:

> There is a profound and genuinely substantial difference between *example(s)* and *ensample(s)* in the AV 1611 King James Bible. Though the words are similar, they are not identical. Though they are plainly akin one to the other, they are not the same. There are distinct and discernable characteristics between them that are manifest in the King James Bible.[44]

In summation, according to Stephens, the words in question are substantively different in meaning within the KJB even though no English Language reference work can corroborate this claim.

Previously, I outlined how there are two different Greek words in the New Testament (*typos* & *hypodeigma*) that were rendered as both "example(s)" and "ensample(s)" by the King James translators (See the table above on page 48). Because Brother Stephens sees a substantive difference in meaning between the two English words, he uses the textual facts outlined previously regarding the Greek to argue that there is advanced revelation found in the KJB that is not present in the Greek.

> Let us face facts: Either there is a bumbling in the translation of the King James Bible, or else the Greek scholars missed something that was not missed in the AV. The two languages set forth **different revelation of knowledge that is not mutu-**

---

43 Ibid., 359.

44 Ibid., 362.

ally consistent. What is revealed in the two languages conflicts, even though, thankfully, no one is going to miss salvation over this matter. But then, salvation is not all that matters, is it, dear Christian? . . . It cannot be both ways in the cases mentioned in this book. The AV translators were fools and blind, insightful geniuses, or the vessels the Holy Ghost used to give us His word. The Greek scholars, who never discerned this matter of *ensamples* and *examples*, are either right about the finality of their understanding and views of the Greek behind these words and others, or they are wrong, and their entire infrastructure of scholarship and linguistic condescension is built upon eroding sand. No middle ground—the Greek is the final authority and the AV is precipitous, or else **the AV reveals, manifest and instructs beyond the Greek**.[45]

Note how Brother Stephens is establishing a false dichotomy between the Greek and the English. Either the Greek is correct or the English (as Stephens has defined the words in question) is correct, but they cannot both be correct. Next, notice how Stephens argues that the "AV reveals" and "instructs beyond the Greek." The implication of Stephens' argument is clear; the King James via its use of the words "example(s)" and "ensample(s)" contains advanced revelation not found in the underlying Greek. Taken to its logical conclusion, this line of argumentation means that the KJB contains additional divine revelation that was not present in Greek, or any other language for that matter, for the first 1600 years of the dispensation of grace. This position is scripturally untenable if God did indeed promise to preserve his word "from this generation for ever" as Palms 12:6-7 assert. If Stephens' position is correct, generations of believers were

45 Ibid., 370-371.

incapable of accurately understanding God's word since they were not aware of the discriminated difference between "example(s)" and "ensample(s)" only found in the KJB.

Stephens concludes Chapter 9 with the following "million-dollar question" regarding the usage of these two English words by the King James translators:

> Again, if the usage of *ensample(s)* and *example(s)* in the AV 1611 is a work of randomness and lack of design, how is it that the King James scholars were really so absent minded that they allowed such an inconsistency to get past them? The proximity of some of the occurrences so nigh unto others and the translators' painstaking review and rechecking of the translation work seem to rule against the ideas that they were merely unaware of their usage of the two words. So then, if the appearances of the two words were not random, then it only followed that this all much have been by design.[46]

Careful readers of Stephens' work will notice that he does not even entertain the notion that the design is found in the translators stated decision to **not** render the same Greek word(s) with the same English word(s) in a rigid manner (See the citation of the Preface to the 1611 above on page 43). Then the voice of the lone English language resource consulted, Noah Webster's *American Dictionary of the English Language*, is dismissed because it does not jive with the author's preconception that "example" and "ensample" differ substantively in meaning. Next, private discriminated definitions for the English words in question are concocted despite zero

---

46 Ibid., 374.

historical evidence that the words even meant anything remotely like how Stephens has defined them. It is exceedingly dangerous to the pro-King James position to argue that words in the KJB can take on meanings that they cannot be historically proven to have had, without a clear defining Biblical passage,[47] just because they are in the KJB.

Later in his answer to the "million-dollar question," Stephens strongly implies that the King James translators enjoyed some sort of "supernatural unction" in their decision to use both "example" and "ensample" when translating.

> One the other hand, what if the responsibility for the actual translation of those two distinct terms as outlined does not reside merely in the academic excellence and the mortal scholarship of the translators? **What if the translators did not cognitively grasp the full depth of the implications of all they translated? What if the Lord actually oversaw the details of the work in a way that the scholars of this hour consider preposterous and heretical? What if God directed the thoughts and mediations and chose to those men in such a way that the translation was not merely the devoted work of spiritual yet intellectual men?** Do we not ask God to guide us in our lives? Do we not acknowledge that while many facet of wisdom and knowledge must be attained by disciple and ex-

---

47 Consider the word English word "adoption" in Romans 8:23 as a case in point: "And not only they, but ourselves also, which have the first fruits of the Spirit, even we ourselves groan within ourselves, waiting for the **adoption, to wit, the redemption of our body.**" No English dictionary defines the word "adoption" as the redemption of the body. Yet the KJB has done exactly that by explicitly stating that in this context the word "adoption" is referring to a specific future event in which the believer's body will be redeemed from the "bondage of corruption" (Rom. 8:21). Unless a clearly definitive verse exists, such as Romans 8:23, ascribing a particular meaning to word within the Bible, manufacturing a discriminated difference in meaning between words misunderstands and misrepresents the task set before the translators. Their task was to formally and accurately state in English what lay before them in their Hebrew, Greek, and Aramaic source texts. Sometimes more than one English word was capable of accomplishing that purpose as in the case of "example" and "ensample."

ercise, that there is still a supernatural unction and anointing that exceeds the mere application of ourselves.[48]

Put another way, how does one not concluded that Stephens is arguing that the translators were inspired to use "example" and "ensample" in specific verses when doing their work. We have already observed that Stephens believes "the AV reveals, manifest and instructs beyond the Greek." Yet he vehemently denies the insinuation that such a position constitutes belief in the notion of "double inspiration" or the idea that God respired His word in English between 1604 and 1611 in the same sense that Paul was inspired when he wrote Romans.[49]

So, what have we seen in this section? Those who are auguring for a substantive difference in meaning between "example" and "ensample" cannot even agree on what the discriminated difference is. Meanwhile, English Language resources that indicate the words are synonymous are discounted because of the false assumption of *verbatim identicality* of wording. In other words, "example" and "ensample" cannot possibly mean the same thing because otherwise the translators would not have used two words to capture what could have been stated in one. The false assumption that preservation/transmission requires *verbatim identicality* of wording has led some to imply, if not explicitly assert, that the KJB is advanced revelation beyond that found in the Greek.

It is high time that we King James Bible Believers cease manufacturing "discriminated" differences in meaning between words,

48 Ibid., 374.
49 Ibid., 378-379.

which don't exist and accept the fact that there are different ways of saying the same thing. Our beloved translators knew this and translated accordingly; it's time for us to recognize it as well.

STABLISH(ED) AND ESTABLISH(ED)

Before concluding this section of the book, I would like to look at two more words over which much discourse has transpired: "stablish(ed)" and "establish(ed)." Once again, Bible Protector Matthew Verschuur stands out as a prime example of someone who maintains that "stablish" and "establish" are different words carrying different meanings. In his *Glistering Truths* Brother Verschuur states the following regarding the difference between the words in question.

> According to the *Oxford English Dictionary*, the main meaning of the word "stablish" is, "To place or set firmly in position; to station in a place." This is not exactly the same as "establish", which firstly means, "To render stable or firm". Consider Psalm 93:1b, 2a, "the world also is stablished, that it cannot be moved. Thy throne *is* established of old". The Psalmist is showing that the world is placed by God, while God's throne has been made to have internal strength to endure for a long time. Although similar, these words have diffcrent meanings, and are used accurately in many places throughout the King James Bible.[50]

---

50 Matthew Verschuur. *Glistering Truths*. 28.

This time Bible Protector referenced an English language resource to substantiate the difference between "stablish" and "establish," the *OED*.

In his series on the *Excellency of Older English*, Pastor Keith R. Blades spends the better part of an hour making his case that there is a "discriminated" and "world of difference" in meaning between "establish" and "stablish." Regarding the word "establish(ed)" he teaches:

> The word establish or established as it's the past tense there in chapter one there [Rom. 1:11]. Establish still primarily has the same connotation meaning to it that it had back during the Golden Age of English. **To establish something means to set up something or set something up if you want to put it that way. The idea is to lay a foundation. You're either setting something up and other things are going take place with it later on, once the thing is set up. Or you're laying a foundation like in a building process and so forth there that you are going to build upon later, once the foundation is laid. You're dealing with an initial process or act that needs to take place for subsequent process or acts to follow. Establish to set something up to lay a foundation; that initial act or process matter.** But stablish doesn't mean exactly the same thing.[51]

As the bolded portion of the quotation emphasizes, Blades defined "establish" as a foundational activity upon with other "subsequent processes or acts" would follow. Furthermore, he clearly states at the end that, ". . . stablish doesn't mean exactly the same thing."

---

51 Keith R. Blades. *A Brief Introduction to the Excellency of Older English*: Lesson 3. To listen to the audio visit: http://www.enjoythebible.org/excellency-of-older-english/ . To view a summation video visit: https://youtu.be/0KJTI6cohH0?t=25m15s

After finding fault among modern dictionaries for leaving the impression that "stablish" is another word for "establish" Brother Blades extols the merits of the *Oxford English Dictionary*. Regarding the *OED*, he states:

> But when you pick a dictionary once again like the *Oxford English Dictionary* that has the etymological information; you need to see where words come from and not only that, but has the history of development of a word and the history of usage of a word, throughout the periods of English. If a word transcends periods, some do some don't.

However; then Blades states the following regarding the definition of the word "stablish" offered therein:

> And when you deal with a word in a dictionary like that you come along, and you find that the word stablish means to render something stable. Stablished. Stable to render something stable to make something to make secure even to strengthen. Those issues. Stabilize. That's the issue primarily. You can see that . . . Stablish assumes that the foundation and the setting up is already there. Stablish assumes that the setting up is already there. The word is used when the context implies or directly asserts or cites destabilizing influences.

So according to Pastor Blades the word "establish" deals with laying a foundation as in an initial process or act; whereas "stablish" deals with stabilizing something upon that foundation. Blades' students are left with the distinct impression that the *OED* supports this "discriminated" difference in meaning.

The problem here is that the very dictionary cited by Blades as his authority for discriminating between "establish" and "stablish" reports that the two words have more in common than they are different. Please consider both *OED*'s entries side by side.

ESTABLISH, *v.*	STABLISH, v. Now *arch.*
Forms: 4 establisse-n, 5 astabilishe, establisch, -ysch, -issh, 6 astablese, establyshe, 4- establish. **See also STABLISH.**	**[Variant of ESTABLISH *v.*]** = **ESTABLISH *v.* in various senses.**
1. To render stable or firm.	From the 16th c (1500s) there seems to have been a tendency to confine the use of the form stablish to those uses in which the relation of meaning to stable *adj.* is apparent, i.e. where the notion is rather 'to strengthen or support (something existing)' than 'to found or set up'. The modern currency of the word is purely literary, and reminiscent of the Bible or Prayer Book.
†a. To strength by material support (*obs.*).	
†b. To ratify, confirm, validate (*obs.*).	
c. To confirm, settle (what is weak or wavering); to restore (health) permanently; to give calmness or steadiness to (the mind).	
†d. *catachr.* To calm (anger), to settle (doubts).	
2. a. To fix, settle, institute or ordain permanently, by enactment or agreement. Sometimes with obj. clause. +Also (rarely) to impose (something) upon.	1. *trans.* To place or set (a material thing) firmly in position; to station (a person) in place. *Obs.* Exc. in figurative context.
†b. To secure or settle (property, privies, etc.) *to* or *upon* persons. *Obs.*	
†c. To impute (guilt) to *Obs.*	
3. To set up on a secure or permanent basis; to found (a government, an institution; in mod. Use often, a house of business).	2. To set (a person, etc.) permanently in an office, dignity, or condition.
4. a. To place in a secure or permanent position; to install and secure in a possession, office, dignity, etc.; to 'set up' (a person, oneself) in business; to settle (a person) in or at a place; *refl.* to obtain a secure footing; also in weaker sense, to take up one's quarters. †Also *intr.* for *refl.* To 'settle'.	†3. To ordain permanently (a law, rule, etc.)
†b. To provide for the maintenance of (persons). Obs. Cf. *settle*.	†4. To set up or found securely (a government, a condition of things). *Obs.*

ESTABLISH, *v.*	STABLISH, v. Now *arch.*
5. To set up or bring about permanently (a state of things); to 'create' (a precedent); to introduce and secure permanent acceptance for (a custom, a belief). Also, to secure for oneself, a gain permanently (a reputation, a position).	
b. To erect into (a rule, etc.). †Also (with *complement*), to secure in a certain condition.	
c. *Card-playing.* to establish a suit.	†5. To bring into settled order (a country, affairs, etc.). *Obs.*
d. *Cinematogr.*, etc. To introduce and secure the identity or position of (a character, set, etc.).	
6. a To place beyond dispute; to prove (a proposition, claim accusation); rarely with personal obj. and complement.	6. To render indubitable, support by proof or testimony.
b. To affirm judicially the validity of (a disputed will).	7. To make secure, strengthen, reinforce.
7. From the 16th c. often used with reference to ecclesiastical ceremonies or organization, and to the recognized national church or its religions; in the early use chiefly *pass.* In sense 2 (esp. in phrases by laws established. i.e., 'prescribed or settled by law'), but sometimes with mixture of sense 3-5. Hence in recent use: To place (a church or a religious body) in the position of a national or state church.	8. To render stable in faith, virtue, etc.

Aside from the fact that the *OED* does not entirely support Blades' suggested definition for "establish" (see bolded section above); it explicitly tells its readers to "See also STABLISH." When one follows the promoting to see "stablish;" the first thing encountered is that "stablish" is an archaic "variant of ESTABLISH." Second, the *OED* specifically reports that "stablish" "= ESTABLISH v. in various senses." Following this last statement regarding the equality between "stablish" and "establish;" the *OED* contains the following statement in smaller font:

From the 16th c (1500s) there seems to have been a tendency to confine the use of the form stablish to those uses in which the relation of meaning to stable *adj.* is apparent, i.e. where the notion is rather 'to strengthen or support (something existing)' than 'to found or set up'. The modern currency of the word is purely literary, and reminiscent of the Bible or Prayer Book.

The notion there is a discriminated difference between these two words is lifted from the fine print of the entry and not from the main definitions offered for "stablish." No examples, in literature for this 16th century use of "stablish" from the Bible (the KJB did not even exist yet) or anywhere else are even provided by the *OED*. It is therefore clear the *OED* does not view the fine print following the clear declaration of the equality existing between the two words as even meriting explication and/or illustration. Yet, Pastor Blades carries the fine print portion of the definition forward while failing to note the *OED* clearly states "stablish" is an archaic from of "establish;" a point for which he derides "modern dictionaries" for. Even if the word "stablish" did possesses a nuanced meaning in the 16th century (ie., 1500s) that does not necessitate or prove that the King James translators intended to make a distinction between "establish" and "stablish" when translating in the early 17th century.

Laying aside the *OED* for a moment, the first known English dictionary was published by Robert Cowdrey in 1604 and is titled *A Table Alphabetical*. It is important to note that 1604 was the same year King James authorized the translation of what would ultimately become the KJB. Therefore, a dictionary produced in 1604 would be a primary source for helping one understand what words meant at the time the translation work on the KJB was being conducted. According to Cowdrey's *A Table Alphabetical* in 1604 the word "establish" meant: "confirm, make strong." Cowdrey's *Table* also includes an entry for the word "stablished" the past tense form of the "stablish." The *Table* reports that "stablished" meant: "sure, confirmed, one made strong" a nearly identically meaning to "establish."[52] So a 17th century dictionary, contemporary to the time of translation process says that "establish" and "stablish" meant the same thing. So, by the time of the KJB translation between 1604 and 1611, according to the first known English dictionary, the word "stablish" had dropped the 16th century connotations identified by the *OED* and had merged with "establish" in terms of meaning.

Other 17th and 18th century dictionaries reveal that the 16th century nuanced difference between "establish" and "stablish" identified by the fine print in the *OED*'s entry for "stablish" had already passed out of usage by the early 1600s. All of these dictionaries identify "establish" as settling or fixing something upon a preexisting foundation in contrast to the notion asserted by Blades of "laying a foundation like in a building process and so forth there; that you are going to build upon later once the foundation is laid. You're dealing with an initial process or act that needs to take place for subsequent process or acts to follow." Please consider the testimony of the following 17th and 18th century dictionaries for "establish:"

---

52 Cawdrey's *A Table Alphabetical* also contains entries for "stabilitie" and "stable." Stabilitie is defined as "sureness, certain, strong." Stable is defined as "sure, steadfast."

- 1656—*Glossographia* by Thomas Blount—"to settle upon a foundation, to make firm and sure."[53]

- 1658—*New World of English Words* by Edward Phillips—"to make stable, firm or sure, to settle, or fix; to set, appoint, ordain or make."[54]

- 1721—*An Universal Etymological English Dictionary* by Noah Bailey—"to make firm and sure, to fix or settle."[55]

All of these uses of "establish" in 17th and 18th century dictionaries are in agreement with the main meanings of the word "stablish" identified by the *OED*.

Moving into the 19th century one encounters two other dictionaries recommended by Brother Blades in his series on the *Excellency of Older English* namely Noah Webster's *American Dictionary of the English Language* (1828) and *An Etymological Dictionary of the English Language* (1881) by Rev. Walter W. Skeat. Webster offers the following definition for "stablish:"

> **STABLISH**, *verb transitive* [Latin **See Stab**.] To fix; to settle in a state for permanence; to make firm. [**In lieu of this, establish is now always used**.]

---

53 Blount's *Glossographia* also includes a definition for "establishment." The word is defined as "A settlement upon a foundation, to make firm and sure."

54 Phillips' *New World of English Words* also contains an entry for "establishment" which is defined as "establishing, settlement, or settling."

55 Bailey's *An Universal Etymological English Dictionary* also contains an entry for the word "establishment" which is defined as meaning, "settlement upon a foundation."

So, Webster's *American Dictionary* further supports the notion that "stablish" is an archaic synonym for "establish." Skeat's *An Etymological Dictionary of the English Language* follows suit in its entry for "establish:"

> **ESTABLISH**, to make firm or sure. . . Sometimes *stablish*; A.V. James 5:8.

Skeat's dictionary, states that the word "stablish" in James 5:8 means the same thing as "establish"; "to make firm or sure." The evidence is clear from a host of dictionaries covering a nearly 300-year time span that "stablish" is an archaic form of "establish" and the two words are identical in meaning.

As we have seen with the other words discussed in this chapter, the so-called discriminated differences in meaning between "establish" and "stablish" identified by Blades break down when applied to other occurrence of the words in question. For example, II Samuel 7 uses the words "establish" and "stablish" interchangeably when identifying the terms of the Davidic Covenant. Please consider II Samuel 7:12-13, 16:

> 12) And when thy days be fulfilled, and thou shalt sleep with thy fathers, I will set up thy seed after thee, which shall proceed out of thy bowels, and I will **establish** (*kuwn*) his kingdom.
>
> 13) He shall build an house for my name, and I will **stablish** (*kuwn*) the throne of his kingdom for ever.
>
> 16) And thine house and thy kingdom shall be **established** for ever before thee: thy throne shall be **established** for ever.

Verse 13 says that God will "stablish the throne" of David's kingdom forever while verse 16 says "thy throne shall be **established** for ever." What God is going to "stablish" forever in verse 13 will be "established" forever in verse 16. What is the most natural reading of II Samuel 7? Given the definitional work outlined above, the most natural reading is to view the two words as variant spelling of the same word. That the King James translators viewed these words as synonyms is apparent when one considers the fact that the Hebrew word *kuwn* is rendered as "establish" in verse 12 and "stablish" in verse 13.

Matters are further compounded when one considers that other enunciations of the Davidic Covenant found elsewhere in the Old Testament exhibit the same treatment by the King James translators. In I Chronicles 17: 11-14 the Davidic Covenant is repeated:

> 11) And it shall come to pass, when thy days be expired that thou must go *to be* with thy fathers, that I will raise up thy seed after thee, which shall be of thy sons; and I will **establish** (*kuwn*) his kingdom.
>
> 12) He shall build me an house, and I will **stablish** (*kuwn*) his throne for ever.
>
> 13) I will be his father, and he shall be my son: and I will not take my mercy away from him, as I took *it* from *him* that was before thee:
>
> 14) But I will settle him in mine house and in my kingdom for ever: and his throne shall be **established** (*kuwn*) for evermore.

Here as in II Samuel 7, the Hebrew word *kuwn* occurs in verses 11 and 12 where it is translated "establish" in verse 11 and "stablish" in verse 12. Then in verse 14 the word *kuwn* occurs again where it is rendered "established" and applied to his throne that God will "stablish" according to verse 12. What more proof does one need to establish the fact that the King James translators did not view these words as possessing a "discriminated" difference in meaning?

Just in case one is not yet convinced that "establish" and "stablish" carry the same meaning within the KJB consider some other places where aspects of the Davidic Covenant are spoken of elsewhere in the Old Testament. For the sake of simplicity, I have limited the verses for consideration to only passages where the throne aspect of the Davidic Covenant is spoken of.

II Sam. 7:13, 16	I Kings 9:5	I Chron. 17:12, 14	I Chron. 22:10
13) He shall build an house for my name, and I will **stablish** the throne of his kingdom for ever. 16) And thine house and thy kingdom shall be **established** for ever before thee: thy throne shall be **established** for ever.	5) Then I will **establish** the throne of thy kingdom upon Israel for ever, as I promised to David thy father, saying, There shall not fail thee a man upon the throne of Israel.	12) He shall build me an house, and I will **stablish** his throne for ever. 14) But I will settle him in mine house and in my kingdom for ever: and his throne shall **be established** for evermore.	10) He shall build an house for my name; and he shall be my son, and I *will be* his father; and I will **establish** the throne of his kingdom over Israel for ever.

Not just within the same passages are the words "establish" and "stablish" used interchangeably to discuss the various components of the Davidic Covenant but across other Old Testament books and contexts as well. What is said to "establish" or "established" in one passage is elsewhere spoken of as "stablish" in another.

The same could be said for the New Testament occurrences of "stablish" and "establish." The Greek word translated "established" in Romans 1:11 is the word *stērizō*. The same word occurs in Romans 16:25 where it is translated "stablish." The Greek word *stērizō* occurs in 13 verses in the Greek text supporting the KJB and is translated "stablish" six times, "establish" three times, "strengthen" two times, "fix" one time, and "steadfastly" set one time.[56] The only other forms of the word "stablish" to occur in the New Testament text are "stablisheth" in II Corinthians 1:21 and "stablished" in Colossians 2:7. Both of these English words are a translation of the Greek word *bebaioō*, which is elsewhere translated as "established" in Hebrew 13:9.

stērizō (G4741)	English Translation	*bebaioō* (G950)[57]	English Translation
Rom. 1:11	established	II Cor. 1:21	*stablisheth*
Rom. 16:25	*stablish*	Col. 2:7	*stablished*
I Thes. 3:2	establish	Heb. 13:9	established
I Thes. 3:13	*stablish*		
II Thes. 2:17	*stablish*		
II Thes. 3:3	*stablish*		
Jam. 5:8	*stablish*		
I Pet. 5:10	*stablish*		
II Pet. 1:12	established		

56 To view the Lexicon entry for *stērizō* visit: https://www.blueletterbible.org/lang/lexicon/lexicon.cfm?Strongs=G4741&t=KJV

57 To view the Lexicon entry for *bebaioō* visit: https://www.blueletterbible.org/lang/lexicon/lexicon.cfm?Strongs=G950&t=KJV

So, as we saw in the Old Testament, the King James translators used the various forms of "stablish" and "establish" interchangeably throughout the New Testament.

Before concluding this discussion of how "stablish" and "establish" are used in the Biblical text it is important to note that Brother Verschuur (Bible Protector) and Brother Blades utilize the same dictionary, the *OED*, to assert that "stablish" and "establish" do not mean the same thing. Yet, they disagree as to exact meaning of each word.

Brother Verschuur	Brother Blades
Stablish—"to place or set firmly in position; to station in place"	*Stablish*—"to render something stable; to make secure even to strengthen; stablish assumes that the foundation and the setting up is already in place; it assumes that the setting up is already there."
Establish—"to render stable or firm"	*Establish*—"to set something up, lay a foundation, an initial act implying later building there upon"

How can this be the case? It is obvious that the supposed difference in meaning does not arise from the words themselves since the *OED* indicates the words are equivalents. What is evidently occurring is that each zealous defender of the KJB has pre-decided that "stablish" and "establish" have different meanings. Since neither the *OED* nor other dictionaries support such a distinction, each KJB defender has had to manufacture a supposed difference in meaning which does not exist. Thus, one observes that they invent different meanings.

The fact that they invent different meanings is proof the supposed distinction between "stablish" and "establish" is not real but contrived.

Given the facts presented in this section, it makes far more sense to view "stablish" and "establish" as different ways of saying the same thing. A host of English language resources stretching all the way back to early 17th century, when the translation work on the KJB was being conducted, report that the words are equivalent in meaning. Moreover, it is clear from the King James text itself that the translators used these words interchangeably in both the Old and New Testaments.

Part I Takeaways

Part I demonstrates how far some are willing to go to protect the standard of *verbatim identicality*. As a King James Bible Believer, I think I understand where these believers are coming from. We are tired of having our Bible attacked by skeptics who cannot accept the notion that an inerrant Bible exists in any language outside of the original autographs. That being said, one should not adopt positions which are contrary to the historical and textual FACTS, because they do not help our cause; they hamper it. If one does not accept "throughly" and "thoroughly" or "alway" and "always" or "ensample" and "example" or "stablish" and "establish;" to be variant spellings of the same word, their rhetoric logically boxes them into a corner mandating they declare which edition of the KJB is the inerrant one.

King James Bible Believers already accept that the various editions of the KJB between 1611 and 1769 exhibit changes in orthography (See Section 1 on Page 2). If believers can accept the 1611 as the inerrant word of God when it spells the same word differently in the same verse, they ought to be able to comprehend that a change in the spelling of "throughly" to "thoroughly" does not constitute a substantive difference in meaning. Manufacturing meanings for words not supported by any known English language reference work plays into the hands of our opponents and practically scuttles our own ship. It is the presupposition of that preservation/transmission occurred with *verbatim identicality* of wording, which causes some well-intentioned Bible Believers to maintain that words spelled differently are wholly different words when in fact, they are simply variants. Variants in spelling are understood and tolerated within the 1611; as well as between editions of the KJB until 1769. Yet, modern printings of the KJB exhibiting further orthographical updating beyond 1769 are viewed as "corrupted" or incapable of conveying the exact sense of scripture. If one can hold that a 1611 edition can be inerrant and convey the exact sense when it spells the same word differently in the same verse; then why would further orthographical changes beyond 1769 automatically constitute "corruptions"?

Not only will this problem not go away for the standard editions of the KJB between 1611 and 1769; but Part II will demonstrate that the problem is compounded when one considers the printed history of the KJB in the United States. As early as 1792, nearly one hundred years before the publication of the Revised Version (1881), American Bible publishers were already "Americanizing" the spelling of words in King James Bibles printed in the United States. If one is going to persist in the belief that KJBs exhibiting these spelling changes are "corruptions" then they must also conclude that generations of unwitting American Christians who used these Bibles did not possess the pure word of God.

Part II

The King's English in the New World: A Brief Textual History of King James Bible in America

The Lack of Uniformity

L ocal Church Bible Publishers (LCBP) a ministry of Parker Memorial Baptist Church in Lansing, Michigan published a small booklet titled, *Have You Seen Some of the Changes That Publishers Are Making in Your King James Bible?* As the title suggests, the booklet seeks to sound the alarm regarding the "liberties" being taken by modern American publishers of the KJB. Three general areas of concern with respect to the King James text are addressed: 1) doctrinal changes, 2) word changes, and 3) spelling changes.

The section on doctrinal changes deals primarily with instances where various printings fail to capitalize the 's' in Spirit when referring to the third member of the Godhead.[58] LCBP does, however,

---

58 LCBP's booklet lists the following references to be checked for text tampering in the KJB:

Gen. 1:2; 41:38

Jud. 3:10; 6:34; 11:29; 13:25; 14:6; 14:19; 15:14

I Sam. 10:6; 10:10; 11:6; 16:13-14; 19:20, 23

II Sam. 23:2

I Kin. 18:12; 22:24

II Kin. 2:16

acknowledge that "there are verses in your Bible containing the word "spirit" with a small 's,' which refer to the "spirit of God." If you study the passage, you will see that it is not referring to the person of the Holy Spirit, but rather to God's spirit or emotion."[59] No other specific doctrinal changes are noted in this section.

Regarding word changes LCBP's booklet reports that "some King James Bibles have over 800 changes, changing ALL English spelled words to CONTEMPORARY American spellings."[60] Readers are challenged to take the provided list of word changes and look up their definitions and consider how the meaning of verses is altered by the new word usage.[61] Three of the pairs of words catalogued as "word changes" include: "throughly/thoroughly", "ensample/example", and "alway/always". Moreover, LCBP reports that in one particular Bible they found twenty-three references where the word "alway" had been changed to "always."[62] These words are viewed by LCBP as wholly different words that alter the meaning of the text not merely a variance in orthographical spelling.

II Chronicles 15:1; 18:23; 20:14; 24:20

Job 33:4

Isa. 40:13; 48:16; 59:19; 61:1; 63:10, 11, 14

Eze. 11:5, 24

Matt. 4:1

59 *Have You Seen Some of the Changes That Publishers Are Making in Your King James Bible?* , 3.

60 Ibid., 5.

61 Ibid., 4.

62 Ibid., 5.

Despite identifying "ensample/example" and "alway/always" as word changes, both pairs of words also appear in the booklet's third section on spelling changes. This section catalogues 95 words whose spelling has been changed by American publishers.[63] Consequently, LCBP is unclear about whether the words in question are word changes or spelling changes. Either way, the ministry's publication views modern publishers as "tampering" with the King James text. The spelling of the English word "Saviour" is used as a case in point to demonstrate the seriousness of these spelling changes.

- **Savior**—"is a six letter spelling and in Bible numerology, six is the letter of man."
- **Saviour**—"is a seven letter spelling, and in Bible numerology, seven is deity or completion."[64]

Webster's Encyclopedic Dictionary from 1959 is quoted to establish a difference in meaning between "saviour" and "savior." "Savior" (6 letters) is defined as meaning "one who saves, preserves, or delivers from destructor or danger" whereas "saviour" (7 letters) means "Jesus Christ, the Redeemer, who is called *the saviour* by way of distinction." It is curious that LCBP would choose to reference this dictionary for a definition of "savior" when Noah Webster's *American Dictionary of the English Language* (1828) clearly identifies the English word "savior"

---

63 Ibid., 6-7.

64 In other languages the spelling of the word "saviour" differs in terms of the number of letters utilized to comprise the word. For example, in the Spanish ReinaVelara "saviour" is spelled "Salvador" with eight letters in Luke 2:11.

with the Lord Jesus Christ: "One that saves or preserves; **but properly applied only to Jesus Christ, the Redeemer,** who has opened the way to everlasting salvation by his obedience and death, and who is therefore called the *savior* by way of distinction, the *savior* of men, the *savior* of the world."

Ultimately, the ministry maintains that these spelling changes are significant because of their potential impact on people who learn English as a second language. According to LCBP, if these believers "are given a Bible published by an American publishing house, their understanding of some verses could be limited or changed."[65]

It is clear from a consideration of these three categories of "changes" that LCBP views them as substantive or altering the meaning of the text not merely orthographic changes in how words are spelled. This notion is brought home clearly in the "Summary" provided at the end of the booklet: "Some publishers put out several different KJV texts that do not even agree with each other. **It is hard to find any American published KJV Bibles that are identical.**"[66]

What is the standard that is being advocated for here? It is none other than the standard of *verbatim identicality* of wording that was covered in Part I of this book. Second, LCBP seems to be under the impression that this lack of identicality in modern American printings of the KJB is a "new" occurrence of recent origin. Mark well that this is not the case.

---

65   Ibid., 8.

66   Ibid., 10.

I have spent a considerable amount of time studying the textual history of the KJB in the United States. After doing so it is clear that from very early on in the life of the nation, American Bible publishers were already making the types of changes to the King James text identified by LCBP. Moreover, it would not be an exaggeration to say that for most of its printed history in the United States the KJB has not been published with anything resembling identicality.

As early as 1792, American publishers were already altering the orthography of the KJB to reflect "Americanized" spellings. In point of fact, there was little if any uniformity in the printed editions of the KJB in the United States throughout the 19th century. In order to understand why these types of changes were permissible in American printings, we must first address a common myth within the pro-King James movement; namely, that the KJB was **never** copyrighted.

Confronting the Copyright Myth[67]

Historically, it has been commonly held by King James advocates, including this author, that the KJB is the only English Bible in the public domain which is not copyrighted. At the head of their booklet on changes publishers are making to the KJB, Local Church Bible Publishers (LCBP) states the following: "The King James Bible is the **only** English Bible whose text does **not** contain a copyright. Any number of organizations may freely make copies of it."[68]

This statement from LCBP is simply not true given the following facts: 1) the KJB was first published in 1611 and 2) the first English copyright statute ever enacted was the Statute of Anne in 1709.[69] This means that along with the KJB all English Bibles published before

---

67 I am indebted to Brother David W. Reid of Columbus Bible Church in Columbus, Ohio for the assistance he provided in the writing of this chapter. Possessing law degrees from Duke University as well as New York University, Brother Reid's "Summary of KJV Copyright Issues" served as an indispensable resource.

68 *Have You Seen Some of the Changes That Publishers Are Making in Your King James Bible?* 2.

69 Jason L. Cohn, "The King James Copyright: A Look at the Originality of Derivative Translations of the King James Version of the Bible" in Journal *of Intellectual Property Law*. (2005): 513, 525.

1709 were also **not** copyrighted including: the Wycliffe, Tyndale, Coverdale, Matthews, Great, Geneva, and Bishops Bibles.

LCBP follows up the factually inaccurate citation above regarding the non-copyrighted state of the King James text by stating:

> That may sound good, but it has resulted in many changes to the text of the Bible. The Bible says of the devil in Genesis 3:1, "Now the serpent was more subtil than any beast of the field which the LORD God had made." If he cannot get you to discard your King James Bible for any of the new versions, he will try to corrupt the very text of your Bible, while keeping the name "King James" or "Authorized Version" on the cover. One may ask "Are these changes that big of a deal?" Remember the warning, "A little leaven leaveneth the whole lump." Galatians 5:9. After you look at the following changes that have been made, you will agree that the serpent has slithered through the doors of a lot of American publishing organizations. **He has begun a new battle for the book he has hated for so long.**[70]

According to LCBP, it is precisely on account of the fact the King James text is not copyrighted that Satan has issued forth this "new battle" against the KJB. In other words, Satan is using the KJB's non-copyrighted status to enact a new strategy to attack the preserved word of God. Once again, this reality is perceived to be a "new" development.

While it is technically true that KJB has never been copyrighted these statements from the press of LCBP are misleading. Strictly speaking, the ministries comments are only correct when applied to

---

70 *Have You Seen Some of the Changes That Publishers Are Making in Your King James Bible?* 2.

the KJB outside the United Kingdom. The King James text resides in the public domain in the United States. This is certainly not the case, however, in Great Britain where the authority for printing the Authorized Version is vested in the Crown. Even the popular internet-based Bible research website Blue Letter Bible acknowledges this fact by including the following disclaimer at the bottom of every page of King James text: "Outside of the United Kingdom, the KJV is in the public domain. Within the United Kingdom, the rights to the KJV are vested in the Crown."

Outside of the United Kingdom, the Authorized Version entered the public domain after the Revolutionary War.[71] These FACTS run contrary to the standard narrative within the King James Only movement. The right or privilege to print the King James text remains under the Crown's authority in the United Kingdom to this day. Moreover, when these facts are followed to their logical conclusion a different and far more instructive narrative emerges.

English law does not view the Crown as owning a copyright or other intellectual property right in the Authorized Version but

---

71 "In the United States, after the War of Independence of 1776, English patents were disregarded. This caused the Authorized Version—still protected by royal patents"—to enter the public domain outside the United Kingdom." Roger Syn, "Copyright God: Enforcement of Copyright in the Bible and Religious Works." in *Regent University Law Review*. (2001-2002):12.

"Since the Bible was not protected by copyrights, only the royal patents remained; upon winning the Revolutionary War in 1776, however, the United States disregarded all English patents, and everything under these patents, including the KJV Bible, fell into the public domain."

Jason L. Cohn, "The King James Copyright: A Look at the Originality of Derivative Translations of the King James Version of the Bible" in Journal *of Intellectual Property Law*. (2005): 526.

instead having the duty to ensure accuracy in its printing.[72] With respect to the Authorized Version, "The king did not own the Bible as intellectual property, but rather had a duty of ensuring accuracy in printed Bibles."[73] Consequently the Crown's responsibility was to ensure that the text of the KJB was printed accurately and with fidelity. The Crown discharged its custodial authority by limiting/controlling who it bestowed with the privilege of printing the text.

It is precisely on account of the fact the British Crown possessed the right to grant or deny printing rights that the KJB exists in the current state exhibited by Oxford and Cambridge printings more than four hundred years after it was first published in 1611. Possessing custodial oversight gave the Crown the authority to decide who would be granted the privilege of printing and thereby limited the number of people impacting the text. Thus, British printings were limited to only Crown approved printers in primarily four locations: London, Oxford, Cambridge, and Edinburgh. Far from being a detriment to its printed history, the Crown's custodial authority has helped maintain the level of textual consistency exhibited by the modern printings put forth by Oxford and Cambridge University presses.

---

72 "[T]he Bible, and books of Divine Service, do not apply to the present case; they are left to the superintendence of the Crown, as the head and sovereign of the state, upon the principles of public utility. But to prescribe to the Crown a perpetual [copy]right to the Bible, upon principles of property, is to make the King turn bookseller: and if it be true, that the King paid for the translation of the Bible, it was a purchase made for the whole body of the people, for the use of the kingdom." Donaldson v. Beckett, 1 Eng. Rep. 837, 842 (1774).

Roger Syn, "Copyright God: Enforcement of Copyright in the Bible and Religious Works." in *Regent University Law Review*. (2001-2002):7-8.

73 Roger Syn, "Copyright God: Enforcement of Copyright in the Bible and Religious Works." in *Regent University Law Review*. (2001-2002):10.

Much could be said about the history of printing in Great Britain especially as it pertains to the English Bible. The translational work of Tyndale and Coverdale was considered criminal activity by the Crown because it was illegal to print English Bibles in the 1520s and early 1530s. This changed when the Crown sanctioned the production of the Great Bible in 1539. All subsequent English translations were subject to printing restrictions including the Geneva Bible, which was originally printed on the continent of Europe by English exiles during the reign of Bloody Mary (1553-1558). In 1561, Queen Elizabeth granted John Bodley "a patent for the exclusive printing" of the Geneva Bible for seven years. In his book *The English Bible* F.F. Bruce reports that Bodley's original patent was extended by twelve years upon his request of Archbishop Parker.[74]

The title page for the New Testament found in the original 1611 bears the following inscription in Latin at the bottom of the page: *Cum Privilegio.* Translated, these Latin words literally mean "with privilege" or "right" that is, with the right of reproduction (Please see the bottom center of the following image.).

---

74   F.F. Bruce. *The English Bible 3rd Ed.* 91.

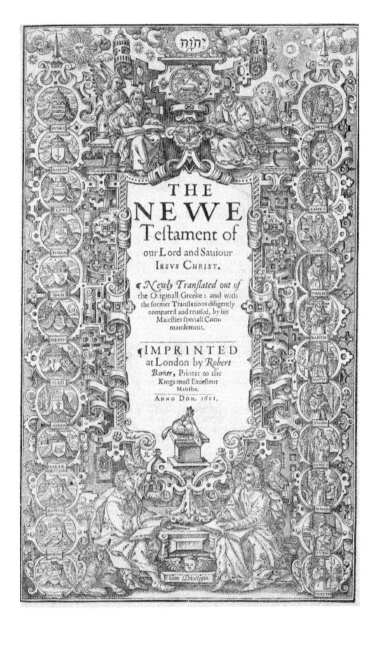

THE
NEWE
Teſtament of
our Lord and Saviour
IESVS CHRIST.

¶ Newly Tranſlated out of
the Originall Greeke: and with
the former Tranſlations diligently
compared and reuiſed, by his
Maieſties ſpeciall Com-
mandement.

¶ IMPRINTED
at London by Robert
Barker, Printer to the
Kings moſt Excellent
Maieſtie.
ANNO DOM. 1611.

Printings of the second edition from 1613 bear the inscription *Cum Privilegio* on title pages to both the whole Bible and the New Testament.

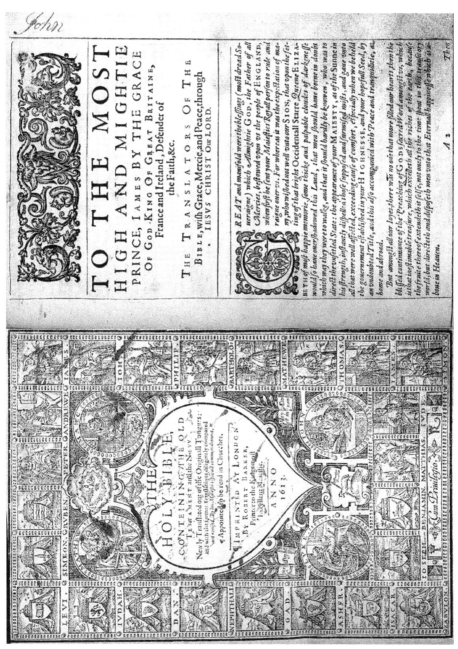

In his 1834 work *The Learned Men: The Men Behind the King James Version*, Gustavus Paine said the following regarding the printed history of the KJB:

> There was no competition for the job of printing the new Bible. It went to Robert Barker, the royal printer, who also published it. His father, Christopher Barker, had received from Queen Elizabeth the sole right to print English Bibles, books of common prayer, statutes, and proclamations. On the death of Christopher Barker in 1599 the queen had given to his son, Robert Barker, the office of Queen's Printer for life with the same monopoly. The Barkers and their heirs held the private right to publish the King James Bible for a hundred years.[75]

Henry Richard Tedder, author of the biographical sketch on Robert Barker in *Dictionary of National Biography, Volume I* wrote the following regarding Barker's exclusive patent to print all English Bibles: "The Bible patent remained in the family from 1577 to 1709, or a period of 132 years. It then fell into the hands of Baskett."[76] John Baskett was the King's Printer from roughly 1709 until he died in 1742.[77]

Some mistake the words *Cum Privilegio* that appear on the title page of some printings of the Authorized Version as indicating that it is subject to some sort of copyright.[78] That is incorrect. Instead,

75 Gustavus Paine. *The Learned Men: The Men Behind the King James Bible*. PDF edition page 97.

76 Henry Richard Tedder. Entry on "Robert Barker" in *Dictionary of National Biography, Volume I*. 1127-1128.

77 Henry Richard Tedder. Entry on "John Baskett" in *Dictionary of National Biography, Volume I*. 1289-1291. https://books.google.com/books?id=Ozc8AAAAIAAJ&printsec=frontcover&dq=Dictionary+of+National+Biography&hl=en&sa=X&ved=0ahUKEwihqMmJ3ZDMAhVBuYMKHXlaAesQ6AEIHTAA#v=onepage&q=robert%20barker&f=false

78 "Patented Bibles often bear the words *Cum Privilegio*, which some laymen mistake as

this phrase refers to the fact that the Authorized Version was printed pursuant to a letter patent issued by the Crown. To the present day, the Universities of Oxford and Cambridge hold active patents for the printing of the Authorized Version.[79] The bottom line for our purposes is this, the British Crown was exerting control over who was printing the text. Implied in this discussion is the following, if Robert Barker, John Baskett, Oxford, or Cambridge Universities wished to maintain their patent to print the Authorized Version they were not at liberty to make textual changes without the risk of losing their exclusive patents. In this way, the text of the KJB was controlled by the Crown despite never having been copyrighted in the modern legal sense.

At the turn of the nineteenth century, the KJB remained under the authority of the British Crown. In his 1965 work *A History of Printing in Britain*, Colin Clair informs his readers that, "the exclusive copyright in Bibles [Note the confused use of copyright in the quotation.] was then (1804), as now, in the hands of the University Presses of Oxford and Cambridge and the Royal Printers, who, at the beginning of the (19th) century, were George Eyre and Andrew Strahan."[80] Philip Schaff's book *A Companion to the Greek Testament and the English Version* from 1884 reproduces a letter drafted May 25, 1881 from Bishop Wordsworth to Lord Selborne which speaks

---

copyright."

Roger Syn, "Copyright God: Enforcement of Copyright in the Bible and Religious Works." in *Regent University Law Review*. (2001-2002):10.

79 "Oxford and Cambridge University Presses and HarperCollins still hold active patents for the Authorized Version."

Roger Syn, "Copyright God: Enforcement of Copyright in the Bible and Religious Works." in *Regent University Law Review*. (2001-2002):12.

80 Colin Clair. *A History of American Printing in Britain*. 250.

to the question of copyright in late 19th century Britain. The letter reads in part:

> I see it stated in some books on copyright, not, however, without some hesitation, that 'the Sovereign, by prerogative vested in the Crown, has the exclusive privilege of printing inter alia the Holy Bible for public use in the divine service of the Church' (Godson on Copyright, p. 432, 437, 441, 454), and that the Queen's printer and the two ancient University now exercised by virtue of patents from the Crown. . . The Queen's printer, who now, concurrently with the two Universities, enjoys the exclusive right of supplying all copies of the Bible (in the Authorized Version of 1611) for general use in the public service of the Church.[81]

So, by 1881, the printing of the KJB had been under the jurisdiction of the British Crown for two hundred and seventy years.

In the 21st century, Oxford and Cambridge University Presses still maintain printing privileges with respect to the King James text. Readers possessing either an Oxford and/or Cambridge edition are encouraged to consult the title page of their respective edition(s). Underneath the coat of arms for each university are the words *cum privilegio* thereby indicating they were printed with privilege and permission of the Crown.[82]

With these FACTS in mind, please consider the following points. First, it is a historical myth to maintain that the KJB was **never**

---

81 Philip Schaff. *A Companion to the Greek Testament and the English Version*. 335. file:///C:/Users/rossb/Dropbox/KJB Class/Throughly/A Companion to the Greek Testament and the English Version

82 Interested parties are also encouraged to read *The KJV Is a Copyrighted Translation* by Doug Kutilek. The author is aware that Mr. Kutilek takes a different position with respect to the KJB than he does.

restricted/controlled in terms of its printing because it remains so to this day in its country of origin. Second, far from being detrimental to its textual history, the very fact that printing the KJB is a privilege bestowed by the British Crown has resulted in the British printings being preserved nearly verbatim over time while many non-substantive textual changes have appeared in printings outside the United Kingdom. The Crown's approved printers were not at liberty to alter text without leaving themselves open to penalties for doing so. So not only is it a falsehood that the King James text was never controlled, it is this very reality which served to ensure the uniformity of the text as it traversed the seas of time and history. The standards utilized by LCBP to prepare their booklet were the texts published at Oxford and Cambridge;[83] both of which were published *cum privilegio* or "with privilege". Without the Crown's oversight of the text one wonders if the twin standards used by LCBP to judge all other printings would exhibit the remarkable degree of conformity that they possess or whether they would exhibit the variety found in the American printings of the KJB.

On this basis, any comments regarding the KJB being in the public domain need to be restricted to printings in America or other parts of the English-speaking world outside the jurisdiction of the British Crown. This of course means that American printers of the KJB have been free to make changes to the text that British publishers were not at liberty to make. Which in turn means that the types of changes

---

83 *Have You Seen Some of the Changes That Publishers Are Making in Your King James Bible?* , 10.

identified by LCBP do not constitute a "new battle for the book" as has been asserted. Rather they are emblematic of the printed history of the KJB in the United States from very early in the life of the nation.

On May 1, 1851 the American Bible Society's Committee on Versions presented their *Report on the History and Recent Collation of the English Version of the Bible* to the Board of Managers. In their report the Committee discusses the state of the King James text as it existed in the mid-19th century after nearly two hundred and fifty years of printing. The *Report* reads in part:

> The English Bible, as left by the translators, has come down to us unaltered in respect to its text; except in the changes of orthography which the whole English language has undergone, to which the version has naturally and properly been conformed; and excepting also the slight variations and discrepancies, which in so long an interval must necessarily arise, by reason of human imperfection, in the preparation and printing of so many millions of copies.
>
> **The exposure to variations from this latter source is naturally greater, wherever the printing of the Bible is at the option of everyone who chooses to undertake it, without restriction and without supervision; as in this country since the Revolution. In Great Britain, where the printing has been done only under royal authority, by the Universities of Cambridge and Oxford, and the king's printers in London and Edinburgh,** the like exposure does not exist in the same degree; although, even there slight variations are continually manifesting themselves between the copies bearing these different imprints.[84]

---

84 American Bible Society Committee on Versions. *Report on the History and Recent Collation Of the English Version of the Bible (1851).* 7-8.

Explaining the Lack of Uniformity:
A Summary of the Early Textual History
of the King James Bible in America

Prior to the American Revolution the colonies were supplied with Bibles in the English language from their mother country Great Britain. Colonial publishers are represented as possessing the impression, that if they reprinted the work, they would be guilty of an infringement of the exclusive right possessed by certain parties in England and thereby expose themselves to prosecution.[85] Margaret T. Hills, author of *The English Bible in America* reports that "a very real obstacle [to printing the KJB in America] was the Crown monopoly restricting the publication of the King James Bible to the King's printers."[86] Likewise, English Bible historian Paul C. Gutjahr states that "the story of publishing the English Bible in America finds its roots in the American Revolution. . . Because of the royal copyright

---

85   E. B. O'Callaghan. *A List of Editions of the Holy Scripture and Parts Thereof, Printed in American Previous to 1860.* v.

86   Margaret T. Hills. *The English Bible in America: A Bibliography of Edition of the Bible & the New Testament Published in American 1777-1957.* xv.

[note the misuse of this term copyright], American printers had never seriously concerned themselves with producing their own English Bibles until political events forced the issue."[87]

While the Crown's monopoly constituted the greatest political/legal obstacle in terms of printing the KJB in the colonies there were other practical and/or logistical concerns as well. First, copies from their mother country were abundant, cheap, and of higher quality than any of the colonial printers had the capacity to produce. There is strong historical evidence to suggest that at one point between the 1690s and 1720s the price for a Common English Bible (i.e., KJB) fell to one shilling.[88] When one factors in the costs associated with typesetting and printing the entire Bible there is no way any colonial publisher could have competed against such a price. Second, publishers printing books with the length of the Bible for the first time would typically do so in serial form by subscription over a prolonged period of time. However, the difficulty in securing enough subscriptions to justify the cost of typesetting the text, not to mention printing, caused these projects to not come to fruition.

Allegedly in 1752, Kneenland & Green of Boston printed an edition of the English Bible in a small quarto size.[89] This unconfirmed edition is also known as the Mark Baskett Bible of 1752, based on

---

87 Paul C. Gutjahr. *An American Bible: A History of the Good Book in the United States, 1777-1880.* 20.

88 O'Callaghan. V. See the footnote.

89 A.S. Herbert. *Historical Catalogue of Printed Editions of the English Bible, 1525-1961.* 272. Two other unsuccessful pre-Revolutionary attempts were made to the print the KJB in America. One attempt was made by Cotton Mather between 1695 and 1710 and the other by John Fleming in 1770.

that fact this edition is rumored to have borne the London imprint of the King's printer Mark Baskett. Regarding this mythical edition O'Callaghan states:

> It was carried through the press as privately as possible, and had the London imprint of the copy from which it was reprinted, viz: "London: Printed by Mark Baskett, Printer to the King's Most Excellent Majesty," in order to prevent prosecution from those, in England and Scotland, who published the Bible by a patent from the Crown; or *Cum privilegio*, as did the English Universities at Oxford and Cambridge.[90]

This particular edition remains shrouded in mystery as no known copy could be located by O'Callaghan or anyone else since 1860.[91] Despite its unconfirmed existence, its legend includes information regarding the forging of the insignia of the King's printer, which speaks to the fact that colonial printers did not dare challenge the Crown's patent on Bible printing.[92]

Thus, one passes through the entire colonial history of the American colonies without confronting a single English Bible printed in the new world. One does encounter, however, a few of non-English Bibles printed in the colonies such as John Eliot's 1663 Algonquin Translation as well as his 1708 Gospel of John published at Boston

---

90 O'Callaghan., xiii.

91 Herbert. 272.

92 Margaret T. Hills in her 1961 book *English Bible in America* written 100 years after O'Callaghan's (1861) also has a discussion on the "Boston Basket Bible" in which she concludes similar to O'Callaghan that there is no historical proof that the Bible ever existed. See pages xv and xvi.

in both Algonquin and English.[93] Moreover, German immigrant Christopher Saur commenced printing the Bible in German in 1740 and finished his task in 1743. After Saur died in 1758, his son printed two thousand copies in 1763 and another three thousand copies on the eve of war in 1776. When the war began much of the latter printing was seized and used as cartridge paper or litter for horses. Saur's daughter succeeded; however, in rescuing the sheets of ten complete copies which she caused to be bound.[94] The Declaration of Independence and the crucible of war would prove to be prerequisites to seeing the KJB printed on American shores.

THE FIRST KING JAMES BIBLE PRINTED IN AMERICA

With the opening of the War of Independence the colonies found themselves cut off from the supply of English Bibles from Great Britain. "By 1777, bibles for sale in America had become scarce. The war with Britain had stopped much of the colonies' international trade, and among the items temporarily lost to the American market place was the English Bible."[95] Sensing the impeding shortage of Bibles, a group of Presbyterian clergyman petitioned the Continental Congress in the summer of 1777 that Bibles be produced on American shores to combat their scarcity and correspondingly high price.[96] Congress responded by calling

---

93 O'Callaghan. vi.

94 Ibid., xiii.

95 Paul C. Gutjahr. *An American Bible: A History of the Good Book in the United States, 1777-1880.* 20.

96 Ibid., 20.

for bids from various printers. Five Philadelphia printers offered estimates that varied greatly in terms of time, type face, and paper.

The entry from the *Journal of the Continental Congress* from Thursday, September 11, 1777 records the finding of the Congress with respect to this petition. It reads in part:

> they have conferred fully with the printers, &c. in this city, and are of opinion, that the proper types for printing the Bible are not to be had in this country, and that the paper cannot be procured, but with such difficulties and subject to such casualties, as render any dependence on it altogether improper: that to import types for the purpose of setting up an entire edition of the bible, and to strike off 30,000 copies, with paper, binding, &c. will cost £10,272 10, which must be advanced by Congress, to be reimbursed by the sale of the books: that in the opinion of the Committee considerable difficulties will attend the procuring the types and paper; that, afterwards, the risque of importing them will considerably enhance the cost, and that the calculations are subject to such uncertainty in the present state of affairs, that Congress cannot much rely on them. . .[97]

After considering the bids, the Congress decided that it would be much cheaper and reliable to simply import Bibles, and so they decided to attempt to procure 20,000 Bibles from Holland, Scotland, or elsewhere in Europe.[98]

---

97 *Journals of the Continental Congress 1774-1789.* Entry for Thursday, September 11, 1777: pages 733-734. To view images of the pages themselves visit the following link and follow the navigation prompts: https://memory.loc.gov/cgi-bin/ampage?collId=lljc&fileName=008/lljc008.db&recNum=359&itemLink=r?ammem/hlaw:@field(DOCID+@lit(jc00897))%230080360&linkText=1

98 Gutjahr. 20.

that the use of the Bible is so universal, and its importance so great, that your committee refer the above to the consideration of Congress, and if Congress shall not think it expedient to order the importation of types and paper, your committee recommend that Congress will order the Committee of Commerce to import 20,000 Bibles from Holland, Scotland, or elsewhere, into the different ports of the states in the Union.

Whereupon, the Congress was moved, to order the Committee of Commerce to import twenty thousand copies of the Bible.[99]

Regarding this resolution to import Bibles from elsewhere in Europe, historian Paul C. Gutjahr reports that "No action was ever taken on this decision, for soon after it was made, the Congress had to flee Philadelphia. This petition for bibles . . . faded into the background forever as the Congress found itself with the more pressing concerns of war."[100]

It was Robert Aitken from Scotland, one of the five printers who submitted a bid to Congress for an American printing of the English Bible who braved the uncertainties of war to produce the first English New Testament in the New World. Aitken who was also Congress' official printer publishing the *Congressional Journal* did not let the decision to import Bibles from Europe stop him from pursuing the enterprise. Given the fact that it required substantially less work and resources to print the New Testament when compared with the entire Bible, Aitken limited his work accordingly. In 1777,

---

99 *Journals*. . Entry for Thursday, September 11, 1777: pages 734. To view the page visit: https://memory.loc.gov/cgi-bin/ampage?collId=lljc&fileName=008/lljc008. db&recNum=360&itemLink=r?ammem/hlaw:@field(DOCID+@lit(jc00897))%230080 361&linkText=1

100 Gutjahr. 20.

he published the first English New Testament ever printed in the colonies. Aitken's risk paid off and was met with great successes, so much so that he produced editions of his New Testament in 1778, 1779, 1780, and 1781. Thus, began the printing of the KJB in what would soon become the United States of American.

In a petition dated January 21, 1781, Robert Aitken announced to the Continental Congress that he had undertaken to print an edition of the entire Bible. On Thursday, September 12, 1782 the Congressional Committee assigned oversight on the "Aitken Memorial;" and gave the following update on Aitken's progress and product:

> That Mr. Aitken has at great expense now finished an American edition of the Holy Scriptures in English; that the Committee have, from time to time, attended to his progress in the Work; that they also recommended it to the Two Chaplains of Congress to examine and give their opinion of the execution, who have accordingly reported thereon, the recommendation and report being as follows:
>
> Philadelphia, 1 September, 1782.
>
> Rev. Gentlemen, Our knowledge of your piety and public spirit leads us without apology to recommend to your particular attention the edition of the holy scriptures publishing by Mr. Aitken. He undertook this expensive work at a time, when from the circumstances of the war, an English edition of the Bible could not be imported, nor any opinion formed how long the obstruction might continue. On this account particularly he deserves applause and encouragement. We therefore wish you, reverend gentlemen, to examine the execution of the work, and if approved, to give it the sanction of your judgment and the weight of your recommendation. We are with very great respect, your most obedient humble servants,

(Signed) James Duane, Chairman,

In behalf of a committee of Congress on Mr. Aitken's memorial.

Rev. Dr. White and Rev. Mr. Duffield, chaplains of the United States in Congress assembled.

REPORT.

Gentlemen, Agreeably to your desire, we have paid attention to Mr. Robert Aitken's impression of the holy scriptures, of the old and new testament. Having selected and examined a variety of passages throughout the work, we are of opinion, that it is executed with great accuracy as to the sense, and with as few grammatical and typographical errors as could be expected in an undertaking of such magnitude. Being ourselves witnesses of the demand for this invaluable book, we rejoice in the present prospect of a supply, hoping that it will prove as advantageous as it is honorable to the gentleman, who has exerted himself to furnish it at the evident risk of private fortune. We are, gentlemen, your very respectful and humble servants,

(Signed) William White,

George Duffield.

Philadelphia, September 10, 1782.

Hon. James Duane, esq. chairman, and the other hon. gentlemen of the committee of Congress on Mr. Aitken's memorial.

Whereupon, *Resolved,* That the United States in Congress assembled, highly approve the pious and laudable undertaking of Mr. Aitken, as subservient to the interest of religion as well as an instance of the progress of arts in this country, and being satisfied from the above report, of his care and accuracy in the execution of the work, they recommend this edition of the Bible to the inhabitants of the United States, and hereby authorise him to publish this recommendation in the manner he shall think proper.[101]

Aitken's Bible of 1782 was the first Bible printed in this country in the English language having an American imprint. The report and resolution of the Committee quoted above was reproduced inside Aitken's Bible following the title page but before the Table of Contents for the Old and New Testaments.[102] Textually, Aitken's Bible conforms to the standard King James Oxford Text of 1769 edited by Blaney.[103]

Before moving on it seems prudent to pause in an effort to appreciate the magnitude of Aitken's accomplishment given the fact that it was the first complete KJB printed in America. Aitken committed himself to setting and proofing type for nearly two thousand pages of text. Moreover, he somehow acquired a necessary amount of paper at a time when paper had to be made by hand or imported from Europe. In appearance, Aitken's Bible was bound in both one and two volume printings in simple calf skin along with some gold-tooled ornamentation. It is also significant to note that Aitken moved away from the common subscriptions sales strategy to a method that involved other booksellers selling his product. He sold or traded copies of his Bible to other printers and store owners who turned around and sold his volume in their shops. Given the astronomical expense associated with printing 10,000 complete Bibles under these conditions Aitken sought to offset his product costs by securing a loan from the General

books.google.com/books?id=JhdOAAAAMAAJ&printsec=frontcover&dq=journal+of+the+continental+congress+volume+4&hl=en&sa=X&ved=0ahUKEwiNqtXp353MAhUks4MKHRYpA4oQ6AEIKjAC#v=onepage&q&f=false

102 O'Callaghan. xxiii.

103 To view a copy of Robert Aitken's 1782 Kings James Bible visit: https://archive.org/stream/1782RobertAitkenKJVBible/1782 Robert Aitken KJV Bible#page/n0/mode/2up

Assembly of the Commonwealth of Pennsylvania and the written endorsement of the Continental Congress found in the Preface to his edition and quoted above.[104]

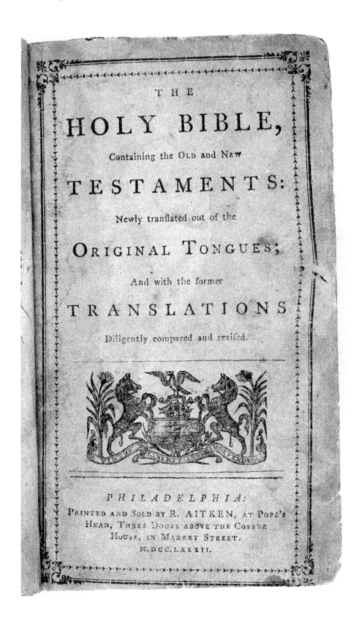

104 Gutjahr. 21.

Despite Aitken's due diligence his timing proved tragic. Almost immediately after the publication of the work peace was proclaimed with Great Britain.[105] Imported Bibles began to flow again into America shores with the end of the Revolution. "As it turned out, English publishers could undersell the price of Aitken's Bible and surpass it in terms of quality, because of the long practice of English publishers and their access to better raw materials."[106] Desiring to avoid complete financial ruin, Aitken petitioned Congress to purchase a portion of his stock to reduce his financial loses. In addition, he approached George Washington with the idea of giving one of his Bibles to every veteran of the American Revolution; in the end neither idea was accepted.[107] In an act of charity, the Philadelphia Synod of the Presbyterian Church agreed to purchase Aitken's Bibles and distribute them among the poor.

> Resolved, as Mr. Aitken, from laudable motives, and with great expense, hath undertaken and executed an elegant impression of the Holy Scriptures, which on account of the importation of Bibles from Europe, will be very injurious to his temporal circumstances, the Synod agree that the Committee to purchase Bible for distribution among the Poor, purchase Aitken's Bibles and no other, and earnestly recommend it to all to purchase such in preference to any other.[108]

---

105 O'Callaghan. xxiii.

106 Gutjahr. 21-22.

107 Ibid., 23.

108 O'Callaghan. xxiii.

Robert Aitken remained in the printing trade until his death in 1802 but never fully recovered financially. There are fifty extant copies of his complete Bible from 1782 that are known to Bible historians.

POST-REVOLUTIONARY KING JAMES BIBLES (1783-1800)

During the seventeen years between the end of the Revolution and the turn of the century four significant editions of the KJB were printed in American. These were the editions printed by Isaac Collins (1789), Isaiah Thomas (1791), the Brown's Self-Interpreting Family Bible (also known as Brown Family Folio Bible, 1792), and Huge Gaine (1792). Other minor printings of the New Testament also occurred during this time period. For a complete list of editions of the post-Revolutionary era interested parties are encouraged to consult Margaret T. Hills' book *The English Bible in America: A Bibliography of Editions of the Bible & New Testament Published in America 1777-1957.*

Advertisements for the editions of Collins, Thomas, and Brown alarmed theologians in the newly formed republic who were concerned with the purity and uniformity of the text. While the core text of these Bibles was the King James text of 1769 it was clear that publishers were already seeking to embellish their editions by adding ancillary material such as marginal notes, references, concordances and the like. As a result, the subject was brought before the Congregational Ministers of Massachusetts at their Annual Convention in 1790. On 27 May 1790 the Convention passed a resolution to be sent to the

Congress of the United States regarding regulating Bible printing in the Republic. The petition reads in part:

> . . . to the Congress of the United States a petition requesting the attention of that Hon'ble Body, to the subject of the several impressions of the Bible now making; respecting the importance of accuracy in these impressions; and earnestly praying that they would take such measure, as the Constitution may permit, that no Edition of the Bible, or its translation be published in American without its being carefully inspected and certified to be free from error.[109]

The petition was read in the United States Senate on June 10, 1790 where it was immediately tabled for future consideration.

In January 1791 the Baptist Associations of New Hampshire, Massachusetts, Rhode Island, Connecticut, and Vermont also submitted petitions to Congress "to adopt measures to prevent the publication of any inaccurate editions of the Holy Bible." Later that same year in December 1791 the First Amendment was ratified and added to the Constitution which stated in part, "Congress shall make no law respecting an establishment of religion or prohibiting the free exercise thereof; or abridging the freedom of speech or the press. . ." Thereafter, all such petitions regarding the regulation of Bible printing in the United States were not acted upon by Congress as they were viewed as clear violations of the First Amendment.

Thus, were the conditions created for the unregulated publication of the KJB in the United States. First, after the Revolution

---

109 *Senate Journal.* 107.

American printers felt no compulsion to heed the British Crown's patent for printing the King James text. Second, on account of the First Amendment the United States government took no steps to limit or regulate its publication. Consequently, it would not be long before Americanized editions of the King James text began to appear in the United States.

MATTHEW CAREY'S COLLATION AND EDITIONS

Shortly after the turn of the century in 1801 Matthew Carey of Philadelphia printed a Quarto edition of the King James Version. This was not Carey's first foray into Bible printing; previously in 1790 he printed 471 copies of the Catholic Douay Rheims Bible.[110] In preparation of the proof sheets for his 1801 edition of the King James, Carey conducted a collation comparing eighteen editions: four London, three Cambridge, three Oxford, six Edinburgh; and two American, those of Isaac Collins and Isaiah Thomas.[111] After completing his collation Carey identified five kinds of variants between the editions surveyed: 1) punctuation, 2) orthography, 3) use of italic, 4) verbal differences without affecting the sense, and 5) variations in both words and sense.[112] Regarding the "Orthographical Variations" Carey wrote:

---

110 Gutjahr. 23-24.

111 Matthew Carey. "Autobiography of Matthew Carey" in *New England Magazine, Vol. 6.* 1834, 230. https://books.google.com/books?id=ZN0XAQAAIAAJ&pg=PA230&lpg=PA230&dq=In+1801#v=onepage&q=In%201801&f=false

112 Ibid., 232.

These are not as numerous as the former; but they are by no means inconsiderable. Among these that attracted most attention, in the progress of the work, were—besides, beside; towards, toward; among, amongst; vallies, valleys; champion, champaign; subtil, subtile; divers, diverse; aught, ought; born, borne; &c., &c.

Diverse and divers are miserably confounded together. They appear to be regarded as synonymous, which is an egregious error. Divers signifies many; diverse, different.[113]

Carey's work from the early 19th century highlights the fact that variations in orthography between British editions as well as between American editions and British printings existed from very early in the print history of the KJB in the United States.

Google Books has a digital copy of an 1813 edition of the King James published by William Carey.[114] According to Margaret T. Hills' book *The English Bible in America*, Carey released two different editions in 1813 from standing type. The first edition was printed in quarto size and contained ten maps, thirteen historical engravings, and Brown's Concordance.[115] In contrast the second 1813 edition printed by Carey did not contain these ancillary materials and answers to Carey's duodecimo edition from 1803/02.[116] Hills further reports that William Carey's 1803/02 duodecimo edition contained an Order of Books for the Old and New Testaments as well as an Account of

---

113 Ibid., 232.

114 https://books.google.com/books?id=sJZFAAAAIAAJ&pg=RA2-PR4&dq=the+holy+bib le+matthew+carey&hl=en&sa=X&ved=0ahUKEwje_aqArK_MAhXszoMKHcZ8D68Q 6wEIPDAG#v=onepage&q&f=false

115 Hills. 39.

116 Ibid., 40.

Dates that preceded the Old Testament text. A Table of Kindred in addition to a Table of Time was also included following the Old Testament. Last, a Table of Offices followed the New Testament.[117]

Therefore, the 1813 KJB furnished by Google Books answers to the 1803/02 edition of William Carey seeing that it was reprinted in 1813 from identical standing type.[118] According to Margret Hills, in about 1803 Carey purchased the standing type used to produce his duodecimo from printer Huge Gaine who had also printed a duodecimo edition in 1792.[119] A comparison between Gaine's duodecimo (1792) with Carey's (1803) reveals that they are identical in terms of their preliminary and ancillary additions. Both editions include an Order of Books and an Account of Dates before the Old Testament Text and a Table of Kindred and Table of Time following it. Moreover, both editions included a Table of Offices at the end of the New Testament. The only major difference is that Carey did not include the Apocrypha in his duodecimo whereas Gaine did.[120]

Therefore, the form of the King James text exhibited by Carey's 1813 duodecimo printing answers to and is identical with his 1803/02 text since they were both produced using the same standing type. Furthermore, given the fact that Carey purchased the standing type used to print his 1803/02 edition from Gaine's who used it to produce his 1792 duodecimo; the form of the text exhibited by Carey's 1803/02 and 1813 editions, represent a form of the King James text

---

117 Ibid., 19.

118 Ibid., 40.

119 Gutjahr. 27.

120 Ibid., 9.

in America that dates from 1792 within fifteen years of the advent of Bible printing in this country.

An examination of the Gaine/Carey Text reveals the existence of orthographical variations in the King James text from the inception of its printing on American shores. Please consider the following evidence of orthographical changes in early American printings of the KJB.[121]

Passage	Standard Text (1769)	Gaine/Carey Text (1792, 1803, 1813)
I Chron. 17:12	*stablish*	establish
I Chron. 18:3	*stablish*	establish
II Chron. 7:18	*establish*	stablish
II Pet. 2:6	*ensample*	example
Gen. 11:3	*throughly*	thoroughly
Job 6:2	*throughly*	thoroughly
Ps. 51:2	*throughly*	thoroughly
Jer. 50:34	*throughly*	thoroughly
Ez. 16:9	*throughly*	thoroughly
Luke 3:17	*throughly*	thoroughly
II Cor. 11:6	*throughly*	thoroughly
II Tim. 3:17	*throughly*	thoroughly

The facts presented in this table prove that spelling changes such as these are not a "new attack" on the KJB as has been asserted

---

121 This table is not intended to be exhaustive of every orthographical difference between the Standard 1769 Text and the Gaine/Carey Text. Therefore, we have limited ourselves to a consideration of the same words covered in Part I of this book.

by Local Church Bible Publishers and other King James advocates. Rather orthographical variations in American printings of the KJB are as old as the printed history of the text in the United States. Were Gaine and Carey seeking to "corrupt" the text? Before answering please bear in mind that during the time period in question 1792 through 1813 there was no such thing as a modern version. There was no textual debate, the critical text of Westcott and Hort had not yet been developed. Codex Sinaiticus (1844) had not even been discovered yet. If corruption was the goal, there were certainly more effective measures that could have been taken to undermine the veracity of the text than to change the spellings of these words. Moreover, as Part I of this book established, there is no substantive difference in meaning between the various spellings of these words to begin with.

THE IMPACT OF STEREOTYPING AND THE AMERICAN BIBLE SOCIETY

The execution of Carey's strategy of maintaining standing type for various sized editions required an entire room to house the preset blocks for a single edition. While it was still cheaper than typesetting an edition from scratch for each printing it remained a costly enterprise to house all the standing type necessary to print multiple editions.[122] In the early nineteenth century a new method of typesetting was introduced called stereotyping. "Stereotype plates of type were made from plaster of paris that allowed printers to print

---

122 Guthjahr. 13.

certain works without having to reset the type every time or keep large volumes of loose type set standing in molds."[123] This process arrived in the United States in 1812 and was immediately applied in the Bible printing industry.

In 1812, the Philadelphia Bible Society acquired stereotyped plates from England from which they printed the first stereotyped book in America. By 1815, publishers were using American-made stereotyped plates to print Bibles in this country. Five years later in 1820, fifty percent of American Bible editions declared their stereotyped status on the title page. "Stereotyping revolutionized American book publishing in the first third of the nineteenth century and no book was so radically touched by this revelation as the Bible."[124]

The formation of Bible Societies as non-commercial printers and distributers of the text also appeared in the early nineteenth century. In the United States, the Philadelphia Bible Society was the first to organize in 1808 after the model of the British and Foreign Bible Society founded in London in 1804.[125] Soon after, many other local societies were formed around the country buying their Bibles from local publishers. Given the need for the production of inexpensive Bibles as the country expanded westward the local societies decided to combine their efforts in 1816 and form the American Bible Society (ABS).[126]

---

123 Ibid., 13.

124 Ibid., 29.

125 Hills, xix.

126 Ibid., xix.

The advent of stereotyping and the formation of the ABS forever changed the production of Bibles in the United States. The ABS sought to utilize the new technology of stereotyping to fulfill the ambitious goal of providing a Bible for every household in America.

> No publisher more enthusiastically embraced stereotyping than the American Bible Society. Using the British and Foreign Bible Society as its model, the Society adopted a vision of encouraging the widest possible circulation of the "Holy Scriptures without note or comment." So central was stereotyping to this vision that the Society initially advertised a mission of providing "a sufficiency of well printed and accurate editions of the Scriptures; but also to furnish great districts of the American continent with well executed stereotype plates, for their cheap and extension diffusion throughout regions which are now scantily supplied at discouraging expense.[127]

By 1820, the Society possessed ten different sets of stereotyped plates capable of producing five different types of KJB and New Testaments. In this regard the ABS was trend setting. The first large publishing house to adopt stereotyping was Harper and Brothers and they did not do so until the 1830s. A normal press run for a commercial printer in the 1820s was around two thousand copies. In contrast, the Society printed 20,000 copies of a stereotyped Bible in 1816, and by 1830 was producing 300,000 copies a year.[128] It is important to note that all of these Bible were copies of the common English Bible otherwise known as the King James Version.

---

127   Guthjahr. 30.

128   Ibid., 30.

ORTHOGRAPHY AND THE ABS TEXT

As the practice of stereotyping expanded the production of the KJB in America, the number of orthographic variants also increased given that there was no uniformity of spelling in the different sets of stereotyped plates produced. Once again, Google Books has a copy of an American Bible Society stereotyped text from 1819.[129] This particular edition was stereotyped by E & J White for the American Bible Society and printed by D. Fanshaw of New York. According to the bibliographic information provided by Margaret T. Hills, it is a reprint of the Society's 1816 Duodecimo sized Bible.[130] Both the 1816 and 1819 printings contain minimal ancillary additions, only an Order of Books in the font and Tables of Scripture Measures, Weights and Money, and Time have been added following the Old Testament.[131] Therefore, the 1819 edition of the ABS text was printed using the same stereotyped plates as the 1816 edition, the very first one printed by the Society.

An examination of the ABS text from 1816 reveals further changes in orthography to the King James text from the Gaine/Carey Text (1792, 1803, and 1813) noted above. Concerning the pairs of words we have been comparing throughout this book ("throughly/ thoroughly", "alway/always", "ensample(s)/example(s)" and "stablish/ establish") it is important to note that only the word "ensample(s)"

---

129 https://books.google.com/books?id=rCkVAAAAYAAJ&printsec=frontcover&dq=the+ holy+bible+american+bible+society+1819&hl=en&sa=X&ved=0ahUKEwjgkuvJ2J_LA hUMWj4KHdEUCGgQ6wEIUzAF#v=onepage&q=the%20holy%20bible%20ameri- can%20bible%20society%201819&f=false

130 Hills. 61.

131 Ibid., 50.

remains unchanged in ABS text of 1816 when compared against the standard British text of 1769. As the next chapter illustrates (see pages 123-129) in every occurrence where the words "throughly," "alway," and "stablish" occur in scripture the ABS edition of 1816 has updated the orthography to reflect contemporary American conventions in the early 19th century.

In order to ascertain the extant of the orthographical changes I have conducted a comparison between the list of spelling changes identified by Local Church Bible Publishers in their booklet, *Have You Seen Some of the Changes That Publishers Are Making in Your King James Bible* and the King James text of the ABS from 1816. The results of this comparison are presented in the following table (An * indicates that an entry was added by the author.). Please note that a blank in the "ABS 1816 Convention" column indicates that it utilized the same spelling as the Standard 1769 text.

Standard 1769 Spelling Convention[132]	ABS 1816 Spelling Convention	Modern Spelling Convention[133]
afterwards		afterward
alway	always	always
apparelled		appareled
armour		armor
armoury		armory
asswage(d)	assuage(d)	assuage(d)
astonied	astonished	astonished

---

132 According to the standard of Oxford and Cambridge University Presses.

133 Modern Convention represents the spellings utilized by modern publishing houses such as Zondervan, Thomas Nelson, or Holman Bible Publishers.

Standard 1769 Spelling Convention[132]	ABS 1816 Spelling Convention	Modern Spelling Convention[133]
baken		baked
Balac	Balak	Balak
basons	basons & basins	basins
behaviour		behavior
behoved	behoved & behooved	behooved
brasen	brazen	brazen
broided	broidered	braided
broidered		embroidered
caterpiller	caterpillar	caterpillar
chesnut		chestnut
clamour		clamor
cloke	cloak	cloak
colour		color
counsellor		counselor
defence(d)		defense(d)
diddest*	didst	didst
distil		distill
Elias		Elijah
enclose(d)		inclose(d)
endeavour		endeavor
enquire(d)	inquire(d)	inquire(d)
ensample		example
fats		vats
favour		favor
forbad	forbade	forbade
fulness		fullness
fulfil		fullfill
furbushed	furbished	furbished
grisled	grizzled	grizzled
heretick	heretic	heretic

Standard 1769 Spelling Convention[132]	ABS 1816 Spelling Convention	Modern Spelling Convention[133]
honour		honor
Esaias		Isaiah
intreat	entreat	entreat
Jonas		Jonah
jubile	jubilee	jubilee
knop(s)		knob(s)
labour		labor
lentiles		lentils
lien	lain	lain
lothe(d)	loathe(d)	loathe(d)
marvelled		marveled
morter	mortar	mortar
musick	music	music
neesings		sneezing
neighbour		neighbor
Noe		Noah
odour		odor
offence		offense
Osee		Hosea
payed		paid[134]
publick	public	public
rebukeable		rebukable[135]
recompence	recompence & recompense	recompense
repayed	repaid	repaid
reproveable		reprovable[136]

---

134 The 1769 spells this word as both "payed" and "paid."

135 The word "rebukeable" could not be found in the standard 1769 text.

136 The word "reproveable" could not be found in the standard 1769 text.

Standard 1769 Spelling Convention[132]	ABS 1816 Spelling Convention	Modern Spelling Convention[133]
rereward	rere-ward	rearward
rigour		rigor
rumour		rumor
Saviour		Savior
savour		savor
sceptre		scepter
sepulchre		sepulcher
serjeants	sergeants	sergeants
shew		show
shewbread		showbread
Sion	Sion & Zion	Zion
sith	since	since
specially*	especially	especially
spue		spew
stablish*	establish	establish
stedfast	steadfast	steadfast
straked		streaked[137]
subtil	subtile	subtile
subtilty		subtility
subtilly	subtilely	subtilely
succourer		succorer
sycomore	sycamore	sycamore
throughly	thoroughly	thoroughly
Timotheus		Timothy
traffick	traffic	traffic
traveller		traveler
to day*	to-day	today
to morrow*	to-morrow	tomorrow

---

137 The word "straked" could not be found in the standard 1769 text.

Standard 1769 Spelling Convention[132]	ABS 1816 Spelling Convention	Modern Spelling Convention[133]
unblameable	unblameable & unblamable	unblamable
utter	utter & outer	outer
vail		veil[138]
valour		valor
vapour		vapor
wilfully		willfully
winefat	wine-fat	winevat
withs		withes
worshipped		worshiped
Zacharias		Zechariah

The preceding table contains a total of 100 words; 95 of which were identified by LCBP and 5 that were added by the author. Of these 100 words that are spelled differently in modern printings of the KJB, 37 of them (37%) had already experienced orthographical changes in American printings of the KJB by 1816. In addition, another 16 words in modern printings exhibit a difference of only one letter. In these 16 cases the letter "u" was removed from words like "labour" so that the word reads "labor."

Many King James Bible Believers utilize Noah Webster's *American Dictionary of the English Language* as an authority for defining the English words found in their KJB. The pro-King James website "The King James Bible Page" contains a KJV Dictionary among its many useful and informative resources. The KJV Dictionary was created using Noah Webster's dictionary to define

---

138   The 1769 spells this word as both "vail" and "veil".

the English words found in the KJB.[139] It is important for King James advocates who utilize Noah Webster's dictionary to realize that it is an "American Dictionary" of the English language. In other words, Webster is informing his readers how English words were used and spelled in America. If one were to take the above list of 100 words and search the Standard 1769 Spelling Convention (British Spelling) in Webster's 1828 Dictionary they would not find an entry for many of the words. For example, if one searched for "heretick" they would not find an entry. Conversely, if one were to search for "heretic" they would encounter various meanings for the word. When one compares American printings of the KJB against Noah Webster's American Dictionary they will see that the spelling changes in American KJBs coincide with how English words were being spelled in America.

When afforded the opportunity due to the lack of copyright and Congressional oversight in terms of Bible printing, American publishers "Americanized" the text by continuing to update the orthography to suit their American readership. How is this any different from what occurred with the King James text between 1611 and 1769? Thus, America's print culture gave birth to distinctly American editions of the KJB from very early in the life of the nation without altering the doctrinal content of the text. Over the course of the 19th century as more American editions were produced further

---

139   In fairness to its creator, the KJB Dictionary does include the following word of caution, "Webster's dictionary is an excellent resource, but it is not infallible. The only way to discover the spiritual meanings of Scriptural words is diligent personal study and reading with illumination from the Holy Spirit."

https://av1611.com/kjbp/kjv-dictionary/kjv-dictionary-index.html

Americanizing of spelling occurred and continued without any uniformity across the printed editions in the United States.

Once again, the facts covered in this section bear out that American editions of the KJB were changing the orthography to reflect American conventions well before the textual and translational controversies of the later 19th century. By 1820 the ABS was using ten different sets of stereotyped plates to produce at least five different sized Bibles, yet even these plates contained spelling variants. What's more is that when one considers the sheer number of editions of the KJB printed on American shores between 1782 and 1881; one will search in vain for any two that are identical in their orthography throughout.

While I cannot speak for every spelling change in every edition ever printed in America, I have conducted a collation and comparison of nine different American printings[140] from 1782 to 1881 with respect to the four pairs of words covered in Part 1. Please consider the results of this project in the next chapter.

---

140 Ten if one counts the Gaine/Carey Text (1792, 1803, and 1813) noted above.

Tables Comparing the Orthography of Certain Words In American Printings of the King James Bible Before 1881

The following is a sampling of how the words surveyed in Part I were handled in American printings of the King James Bible (standard 1769 text) before the publication of the Westcott and Hort Greek Text and the Revised Version in 1881. The following tables are limited to complete printings of the Bible containing both the Old and New Testament. This listing does not claim to be exhaustive of the literally thousands of American printings and editions of the King James Bible produced during the time period in question. The same printings/editions are compared for each word(s). Please also note that the bibliographical information regarding the various printings/editions attached to the first table (see footnotes) applies to all the tables but is only explicitly stated for the first. For ease of reading, the older spellings are in italic.

ALWAY AND ALWAYS

	Aitken Bible 1782[141]	ABS Ed. 1819[142]	Isaac Collins Bible 1828[143]	Edmund Cushing 1829[144]	ABS Ed. 1838[145]
Ex. 25:30	*alway*	always	*alway*	*alway*	*alway*
Nub. 9:16	*alway*	always	*alway*	*alway*	always
Deu. 11:1	*alway*	always	*alway*	*alway*	always
Deu. 28:33	*alway*	always	*alway*	*alway*	always
2Sam. 9:10	*alway*	*alway*	*alway*	*alway*	*alway*
1Kg. 11:36	*alway*	always	*alway*	*alway*	*alway*
2Kg. 8:19	*alway*	always	*alway*	*alway*	always

141 In 1777, during the American War of Independence, Robert Aitken printed the first English New Testament in North America. A few years later in 1782, Aitken published the first complete copy of the Bible in the new republic. Both his New Testament of 1777 and his complete Bible of 1782 were printings of the King James English text.

142 American Bible Society edition from 1819. New York: Stereotyped for the American Bible Society by E. and J. White. This printing was done with original plates from the first ABS printing from 1816. Therefore, should be viewed as emblematic of ABS' inaugural printing from 1816. https://books.google.com/books?id=rCkVAAAAYAAJ&prin tsec=frontcover&dq=the+holy+bible+american+bible+society+1819&hl=en&sa=X&v ed=0ahUKEwjgkuvJ2J_LAhUMWj4KHdEUCGgQ6wEIUzAF#v=onepage&q=the%20 holy%20bible%20american%20bible%20society%201819&f=false

143 Isaac Collins Bible 9th Edition from 1828. Boston: Stereotyped by B & J Collins. Published by C. Ewer, T. Bedlington, and J.H.A. Frost. https://books.google.com/books?id =z05HAQAAMAAJ&pg=PA3&dq=isaac+collins+bible&hl=en&sa=X&ved=0ahUKE wjh4NuQ1J_LAhWF8j4KHX-dBF4Q6AEIVTAH#v=onepage&q=isaac%20collins%20 bible&f=false

144 The Holy Bible published and sold by Edmund Cushing: Lunenburg, Mass. 1829. The New Testament from this edition dates from 1828. This edition was printed from Oxford plates dating from 1784. In other words, it was printed in the United States from British plates. A comparison of this Edmund Cushing printing from Oxford plates reveals complete orthographic conformity with my 1917 Scofield Reference Bible containing the Oxford text.

145 American Bible Society edition from 1838. New York: Stereotyped Edition by A. Chandler. https://books.google.com/books?id=HfVYAAAAYAAJ&pg=PA1223&dq=ameri can+bible+society+old+testament&hl=en&sa=X&ved=0ahUKEwjYsvS3iozLAhXotI MKHcQ6BjE4HhDoAQhAMAM#v=onepage&q=american%20bible%20society%20 old%20testament&f=false

	Aitken Bible 1782[141]	ABS Ed. 1819[142]	Isaac Collins Bible 1828[143]	Edmund Cushing 1829[144]	ABS Ed. 1838[145]
Job 7:16	*alway*	always	*alway*	*alway*	*alway*
Ps. 9:18	*alway*	always	*alway*	*alway*	always
Ps. 119:112	*alway*	always	*alway*	*alway*	always
Pro. 28:14	*alway*	always	*alway*	*alway*	always
Matt. 28:20	*alway*	always	*alway*	*alway*	always
Jhn. 7:6	*alway*	always	always	*alway*	always
Acts 10:2	*alway*	always	*alway*	*alway*	always
Rom. 11:10	*alway*	always	*alway*	*alway*	always
2Cor. 4:11	*alway*	always	*alway*	*alway*	always
2Cor. 6:10	*alway*	always	*alway*	*alway*	always
Phil. 4:4	*alway*	always	*alway*	*alway*	always
Col. 4:6	*alway*	always	*alway*	*alway*	always
1Thes. 2:16	*alway*	always	*alway*	*alway*	always
2Thes. 2:13	*alway*	always	*alway*	*alway*	always
Tit. 1:12	*alway*	always	always	*alway*	always
Heb. 3:10	*alway*	always	always	*alway*	always

	Self-Interpreting Family Bible 1859[146]	Harding's Fine Ed. 1863[147]	Holman's Ed. 1875[148]	Latest Illustrated Reference Family Bible 1877[149]
Ex. 25:30	*alway*	*alway*	*alway*	*alway*
Nub. 9:16	*alway*	always	always	always
Deu. 11:1	*alway*	always	always	always
Deu. 28:33	*alway*	*alway*	*alway*	*alway*
2Sam. 9:10	*alway*	*alway*	*alway*	*alway*
1Kg. 11:36	*alway*	*alway*	*alway*	*alway*
2Kg. 8:19	*alway*	always	always	always
Job 7:16	*alway*	*alway*	*alway*	*alway*
Ps. 9:18	*alway*	always	always	always
Ps. 119:112	*alway*	always	always	always
Pro. 28:14	*alway*	*alway*	always	always
Matt. 28:20	*alway*	*alway*	*alway*	*alway*
Jhn. 7:6	*alway*	always	always	always
Acts 10:2	*alway*	always	always	always
Rom. 11:10	*alway*	always	always	always
2Cor. 4:11	*alway*	always	always	always
2Cor. 6:10	always	always	always	always
Phil. 4:4	*alway*	always	always	always
Col. 4:6	*alway*	always	always	always
1Thes. 2:16	*alway*	always	always	always
2Thes. 2:13	*alway*	always	always	always
Tit. 1:12	*alway*	always	always	always
Heb. 3:10	*alway*	always	always	always

146 The Self-Interpreting Holy Bible New Edition of 1859. New York: Johnson Wilson and Company.

147 Harding's Fine Edition of 1863. Philadelphia: Stereotyped by Jesper Harding & Son and printed by William W. Harding.

148 Holman's Edition of 1875. Philadelphia: A.J. Holman & Co.

149 Latest Illustrated Reference Family Bible of 1877. Chicago, IL: printed by Western Publishing House.

ENSAMPLE(S) AND EXAMPLE(S)

	Aitken Bible 1782	ABS Ed. 1819	Isaac Collins Bible 1828	Edmund Cushing 1829	ABS Ed. 1838
Phil. 3:17	ensample	ensample	ensample	ensample	ensample
2Thess. 3:9	ensample	ensample	ensample	ensample	ensample
2Pet. 2:6	ensample	ensample	ensample	ensample	ensample
1Cor. 10:11	ensamples	ensamples	ensamples	ensamples	ensamples
1Thes. 1:7	ensamples	ensamples	ensamples	ensamples	ensamples
1Pet. 5:3	ensample	ensamples	ensamples	ensamples	ensamples

	Self-Interpreting Family Bible 1859	Harding's Fine Ed. 1863	Holman's Ed. 1875	Latest Illustrated Reference Family Bible 1877
Phil. 3:17	ensample	ensample	ensample	ensample
2Thess. 3:9	ensample	ensample	ensample	ensample
2Pet. 2:6	ensample	ensample	ensample	ensample
1Cor. 10:11	ensamples	ensamples	ensamples	ensamples
1Thes. 1:7	ensamples	ensamples	ensamples	ensamples
1Pet. 5:3	ensamples	ensamples	ensamples	ensamples

STABLISH AND ESTABLISH

	Aitken Bible 1782	ABS Ed. 1819	Isaac Collins Bible 1828	Edmund Cushing 1829	ABS Ed. 1838
2Sam. 7:13	establish	establish	stablish	stablish	stablish
IChr. 17:12	stablish	establish	stablish	stablish	stablish
IChr. 18:3	stablish	establish	stablish	stablish	stablish
2Chr. 7:18	establish	establish	stablish	stablish	stablish
Es. 9:21	establish	establish	stablish	stablish	establish
Ps. 119:38	stablish	establish	stablish	stablish	establish
Rom. 16:25	stablish	establish	stablish	stablish	establish
1Th. 3:13	establish	establish	establish	stablish	stablish
2Th. 2:17	stablish	establish	stablish	stablish	stablish
Jam. 5:8	stablish	establish	stablish	stablish	stablish
1Pt. 5:10	stablish	establish	stablish	stablish	stablish

	Self-Interpreting Family Bible 1859	Harding's Fine Ed. 1863	Holman's Ed. 1875	Latest Illustrated Reference Family Bible 1877
2Sam. 7:13	stablish	stablish	stablish	stablish
IChr. 17:12	stablish	establish	stablish	stablish
IChr. 18:3	stablish	stablish	stablish	stablish
2Chr. 7:18	stablish	establish	stablish	stablish
Es. 9:21	stablish	establish	establish	establish
Ps. 119:38	stablish	establish	stablish	stablish
Rom. 16:25	stablish	stablish	stablish	stablish
1Th. 3:13	stablish	stablish	stablish	stablish
2Th. 2:17	stablish	stablish	stablish	stablish
Jam. 5:8	stablish	stablish	stablish	stablish
1Pt. 5:10	stablish	stablish	stablish	stablish

THROUGHLY AND THOROUGHLY

	Aitken Bible 1782	ABS Ed. 1819	Isaac Collins Bible 1828	Edmund Cushing 1829	ABS Ed. 1838
Gen. 11:3	*throughly*	thoroughly	*throughly*	*throughly*	thoroughly
Job 6:2	*throughly*	thoroughly	*throughly*	*throughly*	thoroughly
Ps. 51:2	*throughly*	thoroughly	*throughly*	*throughly*	thoroughly
Jer. 6:9	*throughly*	thoroughly	*throughly*	*throughly*	thoroughly
Jer. 7:5	*throughly*	thoroughly	*throughly*	*throughly*	thoroughly
Jer. 50:34	*throughly*	thoroughly	*throughly*	*throughly*	thoroughly
Ez. 16:9	*throughly*	thoroughly	*throughly*	*throughly*	thoroughly
Matt. 3:12	*throughly*	thoroughly	*throughly*	*throughly*	thoroughly
Luke 3:17	*throughly*	thoroughly	*throughly*	*throughly*	thoroughly
2Cor. 11:6	*throughly*	thoroughly	*throughly*	*throughly*	thoroughly
2Tim. 3:17	*throughly*	thoroughly	*throughly*	*throughly*	thoroughly

	Self-Interpreting Family Bible 1859	Harding's Fine Ed. 1863	Holman's Ed. 1875	Latest Illustrated Reference Family Bible 1877
Gen. 11:3	thoroughly	thoroughly	thoroughly	thoroughly
Job 6:2	thoroughly	thoroughly	thoroughly	thoroughly
Ps. 51:2	thoroughly	thoroughly	thoroughly	*throughly*
Jer. 6:9	*throughly*	thoroughly	thoroughly	thoroughly
Jer. 7:5	*throughly*	thoroughly	thoroughly	thoroughly
Jer. 50:34	thoroughly	thoroughly	thoroughly	thoroughly
Ez. 16:9	thoroughly	thoroughly	thoroughly	thoroughly
Matt. 3:12	*throughly*	thoroughly	thoroughly	thoroughly
Luke 3:17	thoroughly	thoroughly	thoroughly	thoroughly
2Cor. 11:6	thoroughly	thoroughly	thoroughly	thoroughly
2Tim. 3:17	thoroughly	thoroughly	thoroughly	thoroughly

I do not claim that these tables or this book is exhaustive of every orthographical difference that may exist between the various American printings of the KJB. Rather I have endeavored to use words "throughly/thoroughly," "alway/always," "ensample(s)/example(s)," and "stablish/establish" as a means of framing the discussion. Each orthographic variation needs to be considered individually in order to ascertain whether it is: 1) a different way of saying the same thing or 2) a substantive difference in meaning.

Conclusion

Much more could be said about the textual history of the KJB in America between 1777 and 1881 that is beyond the scope of the current volume. The main purpose of this book has been to address a particular aspect of how the King James position is messaged, discussed, and propagated by its supporters. I believe it is detrimental to the integrity of the position to say things that cannot be supported by the historical and/or textual facts. The truth does not benefit from rhetoric, no matter how well intended, that can easily be proven wrong by a better command of the relevant facts. King James Bible Believers have enough challenges as it is, without adopting positions that expose our flanks to further attack.

From its inception in 1611 the King James text has undergone orthographic change. This process is acknowledged as the normal progression in the development of language. Consequently, differences in spelling conventions are anticipated and accepted when comparing the text of 1611 with the standard King James text of 1769. Yet, no King James Bible Believer views this reality as detrimental to their position.

It is commonly held that the only differences that exist between the 1611 and 1769 texts are: 1) the correction of clear printer errors, 2) updates in orthography or the spelling of words, or 3) changes in punctuation as English grammar became more settled. Yet as was demonstrated in Part I, this notion is incorrect and does not accord with the facts. Wording differences beyond printer errors and spelling do exist between the various editions of the KJB. It is here that we must recognize there is a difference between 1) a different way of saying the same thing and 2) a substantive difference in meaning. The wording differences that exist between 1611 and the 1769 King James text fall into the first category i.e., they are not substantive. They are different ways of saying the same thing and do not undermine the doctrinal integrity of the text while at the same time not exhibiting identical wording. If one does not allow for different ways of saying the same thing and insists upon *verbatim identicality* of wording, then one would be forced to declare which edition of the King James is the inerrant one to the exclusion of all others.

Once the insistence upon the standard of *verbatim identicality* is broken one is free to evaluate the nature of each variant encountered responsibly and ascertain the nature of the difference. Herein lies the distinction between the various editions of the King James and modern versions. The editions of the King James do not differ substantively despite not possessing *verbatim* wording. In contrast, modern versions and their underlying Greek text have changed the wording so drastically that they have altered the substantive doctrinal content of the text. Modern versions err because they report information that is false whereas the KJB does not because the doctrinal integrity of the readings is uncompromised despite their lack of *verbatim* wording.

Once this lesson is learned one can evaluate the various differences in orthography present in the King James text honestly. Part I of this essay sought to establish this point. If words such as "throughly" and "thoroughly" can be proven to have the same meaning than it would be a mistake to call editions of the KJB that change the spelling of these words "corruptions." Words such as "alway" and "always," or "ensample" and "example" or "stablish" and "establish" are not wholly different words of completely different meaning but alternative spellings of the same word.

Part II in turn sought to demonstrate that continued orthographical updates to the King James text beyond 1769 occurred in America from the inception of the printed history of the text in the United States. As early as 1792, the spelling of words such as "throughly" was changed to "thoroughly" not as part of a "new" attempt to corrupt the KJB but in effort to conform the text to American spelling conventions. These changes were being made at a point in history when the King James text was not in dispute or being challenged by modern versions. As stated above, Codex Sinaiticus had not even been discovered yet and it would be nearly another ninety years before the publication of the Westcott and Hort Greek Text and the Revised Version of 1881.

As the tables presented in the previous chapter bear out, from 1783 to 1881 the KJB was never printed with uniformity in North America. Nearly every American edition possessed some sort of orthographical variant when it comes to the four pairs of words considered in this book. If one is going to persist in the position that editions containing different orthography are "corruptions" then they would be forced to conclude that generations of American Christians did not possesses the "pure word of God." This conclusion would be reached on account of the fact that early American printings did not accord *identically* in every word with the twin standards of Oxford and Cambridge.

Is this really the conclusion that King James Bible Believers desire to reach? Do we really want to say that generations of American Christians possessed "corrupt" King James Bibles because they did not come from an Oxford or Cambridge University Press? Is it our position that in order to possess the "pure word of God" in English one must possess a particular printing, from a particular press, produced on a particular continent?

In reality the historical and textual facts are messier than we have heretofore realized. Out of our ignorance of the facts regarding the printed history of the KJB in America, King James Bible Believers have adopted positions that functionally impose our present textual and translational controversies upon bygone generations of Americans who knew nothing of the challenges we face today. For them the text of the Bible was not in dispute, everyone clung to the standard of the Common English text, i.e., the King James Bible. It never occurred to them that they might not have God's preserved word if they didn't possess a Bible printed on an Oxford or Cambridge University Press, assuming one was even available to them. They just believed that whichever copy of the KJB they were fortunate enough to possess was the word of God and allowed it to work in them effectually (I Thess. 2:13).

The entire process of researching and preparing this book has been an eye opening and sobering experience. Much that has been written in pro-King James literature in defense of the position, possesses a superficial appeal, but is nonetheless incorrect. As King James Bible Believers, we need to make sure that we are applying the Berean principal (Acts 17:11) to our position on the Bible, and search things out to make sure they are so. Empty, unsound, and incorrect rhetoric does not help our position; it harms it. Therefore, it is incumbent upon believers who stand for the infallibility of the King James Bible to enunciate a position which is accurate and in accordance with the historical and textual facts.

Works Cited

AUDIO

Blades, Keith R. A Brief Introduction to the Excellency of Older English. Enjoy the Bible Ministries. http://www.enjoythebible.org/excellency-of-older-english/

DICTIONARIES & ENGLISH LANGUAGE RESOURCES (LISTED BY DATE)

1604—*A Table Alphabetical* by Robert Cawdrey. http://www.library.utoronto.ca/utel/ret/cawdrey/cawdrey0.html

1616—*English Expositor* by John Bullokar. To view the 12th Edition for 1719 visit: https://books.google.com/books?id=R8IDAAAAQAAJ&printsec=frontcover&source=gbs_ge_summary_r&cad=0#v=onepage&q&f=false

1623—*English Dictionary* by Henry Cockeram. http://babel.hathitrust.org/cgi/pt?id=wu.89104407572;view=1up;seq=10

1656—*Glossographia* by Thomas Blount. https://books.google.com/books?id=8jYP-B1Q9a-0C&printsec=frontcover&source=gbs_ge_summary_r&cad=0#v=onepage&q&f=-false

1658—*New World of English Words* by Edward Phillips. To view the 3rd Edition from 1720 visit: https://archive.org/details/The_New_World_of_English_Words_Or_A_General_Dictionary

1676—An English Dictionary by Elisha Coles. https://books.google.com/books?id=2p-Jh0QbbeakC&printsec=frontcover&source=gbs_ge_summary_r&cad=0#v=onep-age&q&f=false

1699—*Dictionary of the Terms Ancient and Modern of the Canting Crew* by B.E. Gent. https://archive.org/stream/newdictionaryoft00begeuoft#page/n3/mode/2up

1721—*An Universal Etymological English Dictionary* by Noah Bailey. To view a 1763 printing visit: https://archive.org/details/universaletymolo00bail

1755—*A Dictionary of the English Language* by Samuel Johnson. http://johnsonsdictionary-online.com/

1818—*Crabb's English Synonyms* by George Crabb. To view the enlarged 1st edition from 1826 visit: https://books.google.com/books?id=NZtWAAAAcAAJ&printsec=front-cover&source=gbs_ge_summary_r&cad=0#v=onepage&q&f=false

1828—*American Dictionary of the English Language* by Noah Webster. http://webstersdic-tionary1828.com/

1828—*A Dictionary of the English Language* by Samuel Johnson, John Walker, Robert S. Jameson (This is a British dictionary published the same year as Webster's work in America.) https://books.google.com/books?id=z3kKAAAAIAAJ&printsec=front-cover&source=gbs_ge_summary_r&cad=0#v=onepage&q&f=false

1890—*Synonyms Discriminated: A Dictionary of Synonymous Words in the English Language* by Charles John Smith. https://archive.org/details/synonymsdiscrimi00smituoft

1881—*An Etymological Dictionary of the English Language* by Rev. Walter W. Skeat. To view the 2nd edition from 1883 visit: https://archive.org/stream/etymologicaldict00skeauoft#page/192/mode/2up

1989—*Oxford English Dictionary 2nd Edition*

WRITTEN WORKS

American Bible Society Committee on Versions. *Report on the History and Recent Collation of the English Version of the Bible (1851).*

Bruce, F.F. *The English Bible 3rd Ed.*

Carey, Matthew. "Autobiography of Matthew Carey" in *New England Magazine, Vol. 6.* 1834. https://books.google.com/books?id=ZN0XAQAAIAA-J&pg=PA230&lpg=PA230&dq=In+1801#v=onepage&q=In%20 1801&f=false

Clair, Colin. *A History of American Printing in Britain.*

Gutjahr, Paul C. *An American Bible: A History of the Good Book in the United States, 1777-1880.*

Have You Seen Some of the Changes That Publishers Are Making in Your King James Bible? Local Church Bible Publishers.

Herbert, A.S. *Historical Catalogue of Printed Editions of the English Bible, 1525-1961.*

Hills, Margaret T. *The English Bible in America: A Bibliography of Edition of the Bible & the New Testament Published in American 1777-1957.*

Journals of the Continental Congress 1774-1789. https://memory.loc.gov/cgi-bin/

query/r?ammem/hlaw:@field(DOCID+@lit(jc00897))

King James Translators. *Preface: The Translates to the Reader.*

Norton, David. *A Textual History of the King James Bible.* Cambridge University Press, 2004.

O'Callaghan, E.B. *A List of Editions of the Holy Scripture and Parts Thereof, Printed in American Previous to 1860.*

Paine, Gustavus. *The Learned Men: The Men Behind the King James Bible.* http://www.earnestlycontendingforthefaith.com/Books/GustavusSPaine/GustavusPaineTheMenBehindTheKingJamesBible.pdf

Stephens, Kyle. *The Certainty of the Words: How the King James Bible Resolves the Ambiguity of the Original Languages.* Miamitown, OH: DayStar Publishing, 2012.

Schaff, Philip. *A Companion to the Greek Testament and the English Version.* https://archive.org/details/companiontogreek00scha/page/n6

Tedder, Henry Richard. *Dictionary of National Biography, Volume I.* https://books.google.com/books?id=Ozc8AAAAIAAJ&printsec=frontcover&dq=Dictionary+of+National+Biography&hl=en&sa=X&ved=0ahUKEwihqM-mJ3ZDMAhVBuYMKHXlaAesQ6AEIHTAA#v=onepage&q=robert%20barker&f=false

Verschuur, Matthew. *Glistering Truths: Distinctions in Bible Words.* http://www.bibleprotector.com/glistering_truths.pdf

Dispensational Publishing House is striving to become the go-to source for Bible-based materials from the dispensational perspective.

Our goal is to provide high-quality doctrinal and worldview resources that make dispensational theology accessible to people at all levels of understanding.

Visit our blog regularly to read informative articles from both known and new writers.

And please let us know how we can better serve you.

Dispensational Publishing House, Inc.
PO Box 3181
Taos, NM 87571

Call us toll free 844-321-4202

www.DispensationalPublishing.com

CPSIA information can be obtained
at www.ICGtesting.com
Printed in the USA
JSHW020714180420
5144JS00003B/32